27

B
a
w

—

—

D1394928

WILKIE COLLINS

PETER ACKROYD

Chatto & Windus
LONDON

Published by Chatto & Windus 2012

2 4 6 8 10 9 7 5 3 1

First published in Great Britain in 2012 by
Chatto & Windus
Random House, 20 Vauxhall Bridge Road,
London SW1V 2SA
www.randomhouse.co.uk

Addresses for companies within The Random House Group Limited can be found at:
www.randomhouse.co.uk/offices.htm

The Random House Group Limited Reg. No. 954009

A CIP catalogue record for this book
is available from the British Library

ISBN 9780701169909

The Random House Group Limited supports The Forest Stewardship Council (FSC®), the
leading international forest certification organisation. Our books carrying the FSC label are
printed on FSC® certified paper. FSC is the only forest certification scheme endorsed by
the leading environmental organisations, including Greenpeace. Our paper procurement
policy can be found at www.randomhouse.co.uk/environment

Typeset in Adobe Garamond by Palimpsest Book Production Limited,
Falkirk, Stirlingshire
Printed and bound by
CPI Group (UK) Ltd, Croydon, CR0 4YY

CONTENTS

List of Illustrations

TAVISTOCK HOUSE THEATRE.

UNDER THE MANAGEMENT OF MR. CHARLES DICKENS.

On Twelfth Night, Tuesday, January 6th, 1857, AT A QUARTER BEFORE 8 O'CLOCK, will be presented

AN ENTIRELY NEW

ROMANTIC DRAMA, IN THREE ACTS, BY MR. WILKIE COLLINS,

CALLED

THE FROZEN DEEP.

The Machinery and Properties by MR. IRELAND, *of the Theatre Royal, Adelphi.* *The Dresses by* MESSRS. NATHAN, *of Titchbourne Street, Haymarket.* *Perruquier,* MR. WILSON, *of the Strand.*

THE PROLOGUE WILL BE DELIVERED BY MR. JOHN FORSTER.

CAPTAIN EBSWORTH, *of The Sea Mew*	MR. EDWARD PIGOTT.
CAPTAIN HELDING, *of The Wanderer*	MR. ALFRED DICKENS.
LIEUTENANT CRAYFORD	MR. MARK LEMON.
FRANK ALDERSLEY	MR. WILKIE COLLINS.
RICHARD WARDOUR	MR. CHARLES DICKENS.
LIEUTENANT STEVENTON	MR. YOUNG CHARLES.
JOHN WANT, *Ship's Cook*	MR. AUGUSTUS EGG, A.R.A.
BATESON } *Two of The Sea Mew's People*	{ MR. EDWARD HOGARTH.
DARKER }	{ MR. FREDERICK EVANS.

(OFFICERS AND CREWS OF THE SEA MEW AND WANDERER.)

MRS. STEVENTON	MISS HELEN.
ROSE EBSWORTH	MISS KATE.
LUCY CRAYFORD	MISS HOGARTH.
CLARA BURNHAM	MISS MARY.
NURSE ESTHER	MRS. WILLS.
MAID	MISS MARTHA.

THE SCENERY AND SCENIC EFFECTS OF THE FIRST ACT, BY MR. TELBIN.

THE SCENERY AND SCENIC EFFECTS OF THE SECOND AND THIRD ACTS, BY MR. STANFIELD, R.A.

ASSISTED BY MR. DANSON.

THE ACT-DROP, ALSO BY MR. STANFIELD, R.A.

AT THE END OF THE PLAY, HALF-AN-HOUR FOR REFRESHMENT.

To Conclude with MRS. INCHBALD'S *Farce, in Two Acts, of*

ANIMAL MAGNETISM.

(THE SCENE IS LAID IN SEVILLE.)

THE DOCTOR	MR. CHARLES DICKENS.
PEDRILLO	MR. MARK LEMON.
THE MARQUIS DE LA GUARDIA	MR. YOUNG CHARLES.
GREGORIO	MR. WILKIE COLLINS.
CAMILLA	MISS KATE.
JACINTHA	MISS HOGARTH.

Musical Composer and Conductor of the Orchestra—Mr. FRANCESCO BERGER, who will preside at the Piano.

CARRIAGES MAY BE ORDERED AT HALF-PAST ELEVEN.

GOD SAVE THE QUEEN!

Playbill for the opening performance of *The Frozen Deep*
at Tavistock House, January 1857

The Omni

The peculiar appearance of Mr Wilkie Collins made him stand out in an 'omni', as the London bus was frequently called. At five feet and six inches he was relatively short even for the 1850s and 1860s. His head was too large for his body; his arms and his legs were a little too short, while his hands and feet were too small and considered to be 'rather like a woman's'. There was a large bump on his right temple as a result of a gynaecological accident; it was sometimes called 'a swelling of the frontal bone'.

He was always aware of his oddity and declared that nature had in his case been 'a bad artist'; he believed that his high shoulders, and his generally broad body, were 'quite out of all proportion' to his large and intellectual head. He was extremely short-sighted, and always wore spectacles. In his thirties he grew a beard, thus lending much-needed symmetry to his face. In his published work he often draws attention to physical abnormalities that give a clue to distinctive character; he was very interested in what was then the science of physiognomy, but he also mentions among other ailments epilepsy, spinal defects, facial deformities, and paralysis of the limbs.

His friend, Holman-Hunt, gave an account of his demeanour. When welcoming a guest he would rock himself backwards and forwards while clasping his knees, and 'ask with deep concern where you came from last'. Someone else described 'a nervous movement of his knees, as if he were soothing invisible babies'. He could not stay still. When he sensed an attack of gout coming on, an ailment that afflicted him for much of his life, his response was 'his fidgeting with one foot upon the floor'. When in repose, however, his face had a dreaming or reflective aspect; but in conversations his bright eyes behind his gold-rimmed spectacles fixed you like gimlets.

He wore colourful clothes, like many of his contemporaries, as if playing a certain part in the great general drama of life. His doctor, Frank Beard, explained that he would sometimes sit down to dinner 'in a light camel hair or tweed suit, with a broad pink or blue striped shirt, and perhaps a red tie'. When photographed in New York, on a reading tour, he was dressed in a florid fur coat. He was recorded wearing 'a linen shirt dashed with great, gory squares, cut low in the neck, and held together with a rakishly tied Belcher scarf' together with a bright blue jacket and waistcoat. He also owned a range of cravats, striped and spotted. Out for a walk in London one afternoon in his late fifties, wearing a smart paletot coat usually reserved for young men, he overheard a woman say to her companion, 'To think of a man wearing such a coat as that – at *his* time of life!' Yet his preferred costume, when he was working quietly at home, was a dressing gown.

He was universally known for his amiability and general good humour; he was perhaps the sweetest-tempered of all the Victorian novelists. He did not have the hard and driven quality of Charles Dickens; he did not have the brooding and majestic air of George Eliot. He was 'the least *posé* public man I ever met', according to one companion; he was kind and ever approachable. He had no 'side', and seems to have been adored by the women of his acquaintance for his sly sense of fun and effortless charm. He set men at their ease with his cheerfulness and what was described as 'the buoyancy of a youthful spirit'. He said of himself that dignity was not part of his nature. His description of one of his characters might be applied to him, that he was one of those men 'whom everybody shakes hands with, and nobody bows to, on a first introduction'. He was always known simply as Wilkie, not as Collins or Mr Collins.

The bus was known as the 'omni' because it catered for everyone, and thus can be seen as an indispensable preliminary to the Parliamentary Reform Acts of 1867 and 1870. He liked to ride on the omnibus because he wished to immerse himself in what he called 'the Actual', as opposed to 'the Ideal'. Among the routes adjoining his neighbourhood he might have taken that from the Yorkshire Stingo at Paddington to the Bank of England, passing along the New Road (now known as the Marylebone Road), Somers Town and the City Road.

It was a relatively expensive mode of transport – a shilling for a full ticket – but newspapers and magazines were provided free of charge. The bus could accommodate twenty-two passengers and Collins once wrote that 'an omnibus has always appeared to be a perambulatory exhibition room of the eccentricities of human nature'; he liked to scrutinise 'merely the different methods of getting into the vehicle and taking their seats, adopted by different people'. He saw the fashionable young woman in intensely dyed crinoline; he saw the banker, dressed in clerical black, wearing a stovepipe hat. He observed the stout gentleman in a white neckcloth, and the 'shabby-genteel' man with a green bag. He may have noticed how the stout gentleman gave a poke to the 'cad', or conductor, with his umbrella for some infringement of the rules. He saw all the anxious, nervous, exhausted and ailing people of the city. In one of his novels, *Basil*, a young man falls helplessly in love with a girl he has glimpsed on the 'omni'.

One reviewer described his fiction as 'stuffed full' with incidents 'as an omnibus is with passengers on a rainy day'. Safely ensconced in his seat he would have heard all the phrases of the age. It struck me all of a heap. I am dead beat. He was in a blue funk. I hardly know whether I'm on my head or my heels. He's spooney enough to like lemonade. He's a rum'un. That shook him up a bit. Tuck in. Ta-ta, sergeant, ta-ta.

He knew the route of the Paddington omnibus by heart, since for most of his life he lived in the neighbourhood of the New Road. Like most Londoners of the period he remained in the area with which he was familiar. Londoners had some inner guide to the nature of their terrain; they knew where to find the dry soil or the damp soil; they knew of the windy quarters and the sultry quarters; they recognised which neighbourhoods were healthy, and which were diseased.

He lived, apart from some residences of his childhood years, in a small patch of territory bounded by Oxford Street in the south and Regent's Park in the north; the western frontier lies on the Edgware Road and the eastern is formed by Great Portland Street. Scenes from this territory are to be found in much of his fiction, with the immediate neighbourhood of Regent's Park as a particular attraction. Marylebone is in fact one of the most respectable, and also one of the most dreary, areas of London. Most of it is resolutely bourgeois, with solid stuccoed or red brick houses ranged along grimly patterned streets. Yet Collins, of all people, realised that strange crimes and furtive passions might lie concealed behind the brick and the plaster.

The most sensational crimes of the 1860s involved fraud, or blackmail, or poison, where a respectable façade was most important; these were also the issues that arrested Collins's attention. Thomas Hardy characterised the most successful fiction of the period as containing 'murder, blackmail, illegitimacy, impersonation, eavesdropping, multiple secrets, a suggestion of bigamy, amateur and professional detectives'. It is the best possible summary of the art of Wilkie Collins. He celebrated what he described, in *The Woman in White*, as 'the idea of something hidden below the surface'. In the process he created a fragile world racked with nervous tension, where the conventions of ordinary life concealed the burden of secrets and of irregular relationships. This was a world of confused identities, both sexual and social, in which no one had a secure home. This was the world of London.

2

The Family

He came into the Marylebone world on 8 January 1824; his place of birth was a house in New Cavendish Street, and he returned to that street with a mistress thirty-five years later. He was baptised at the parish church of St Mary-Le-Bone with the name of William Wilkie Collins, and throughout his childhood was known as Willy. It may be on the occasion of his baptism that his godfather, the painter Sir David Wilkie, astonished the family by peering into the baby's eyes and exclaiming that 'he sees!'. As Collins remarked later, Sir David Wilkie was more familiar with puppies and kittens than with infants.

The house in New Cavendish Street was shared with his paternal grandmother and uncle; since the Victorians were preoccupied with theories of heredity, and of acquired characteristics, it may be worth tracing Collins's own ancestry. It was believed in the family that they were descended from Samuel Collins, a seventeenth-century anatomist, and from the same family as William Collins, the once celebrated eighteenth-century poet. A more immediate influence may be found in his paternal grandfather, William Collins the elder. He was a native of County Wicklow but, like other young and hopeful Irishmen, he came to London to make his fortune; he fancied himself to be a poet, on the model of his supposed famous ancestor, but was obliged to earn a more prosaic living by setting up as a restorer and picture dealer in Bolsover Street, Marylebone. This was the street to which Wilkie Collins would later bring a second mistress. Thus is the web of London formed.

William Collins the elder, according to his grandson, was not daunted by his relative lack of success. He wrote 'articles in the public journals, songs, fugitive pieces' as well as sermons and even a political pamphlet. His most significant production, however, was a narrative upon the travels and travails of a stolen painting. *Memoirs of a Picture* is a rambling and picaresque account of the world of thieves and forgers which Wilkie Collins himself came to relish. It provided the milieu which he borrowed for a tale of an art forger entitled *A Rogue's Life*.

Yet the elder Collins was never able to free himself from what his grandson called 'pecuniary embarrassment', and the Collins family grew up in the shadow of poverty. When Collins died in 1812 he left his wife and two sons with nothing in the world; Mrs Collins was obliged to sell her furniture and her household possessions, and the family was reduced to eating 'scanty meals' off an old box rather than a table. This penury forced the young William Collins to earn his bread by hard work as a jobbing artist. It may also account for Wilkie Collins's own caution and even parsimony in matters of finance. He was used to bickering with waiters and cab drivers.

William Collins, the father of Wilkie Collins, was twenty-three at the time of his parent's death. He had been admitted to the Royal Academy Schools five years earlier, and had already shown landscape paintings at the Academy's Summer Exhibition. He was now obliged to support his family and, with a combination of probity and hard work, he slowly made his way. He wrote in his diary that 'as it is impossible to rise in the world without connection, connection I must have'. He sought out rich and influential patrons; he became the epitome of respectability and propriety; he was a fervent Christian who was outraged when he saw a neighbour nailing some nectarine trees to a wall on a Sunday. Yet social and professional anxieties were never very far away; this was an age in which it was all too easy to 'break' and to go under.

The solution was industry, dedication and unremitting hard work; in this respect, at least, his son would follow his example.

William Collins first acquired his reputation with *The Sale of the Pet Lamb*, a tender and harmonious interpretation of what in reality would have been a distressing occasion; the lamb was, after all, being sold to a butcher. You might be forgiven for thinking that the affecting scene was an aspect of some rural idyll, with the painter exhibiting what his son later called 'simple yet impressive pathos'. It sets the characteristic tone of William Collins's work in which sentiment was combined with naturalism.

The titles of the paintings convey much of their effect, and of their effectiveness, with a public that chose to conceal or repress the less palatable aspects of English life. *The Burial Place of a Favourite Bird, Cottage Children, Blowing Bubbles* and *The Kitten Deceived* do not convey the mood of a society already agitated by political discontent and economic distress. Wilkie Collins, in a memoir of his father, noted that the painter never depicted the 'fierce miseries' or the 'coarse contentions' that make up a part of life; he chose instead to portray amiable and light-hearted rustics, and to portray in the natural world all that was 'pure' and 'tranquil'.

In 1821, when his income and reputation were secure, he asked Harriet Geddes to become his wife. They had met seven years before, at a ball in Salisbury, but an impoverished young artist could hardly support a family. Harriet Geddes herself came from an artistic milieu. Her sister, Margaret, became a significant and popular artist who in her lifetime exhibited 147 paintings at the Royal Academy. Harriet herself had ambitions to go on to the stage, but this was not considered to be an ideal vocation. Instead she became a governess. But then, in the autumn of 1822, they were married in the English Episcopal chapel in Edinburgh. They were married in Scotland because of the complications of a new Marriage Act that had just come into force in England; this Act was designed 'for the better prevention of clandestine marriages', but its provisions caused such uncertainty that it was abolished in the following year. Wilkie Collins arrived sixteen months after their union.

He wrote later that his mother was 'a woman of remarkable mental culture' who bestowed upon him 'whatever of poetry and imagination there may be in my character'. He said on another occasion that he had inherited her 'spirits'. She was undoubtedly sociable and sharp-witted, with that independence of temperament that her son gave to his favourite heroines. He described a governess in one of his novels, *No Name*, as 'a woman who looked capable of sending any parents in England to the right-about, if they failed to rate her at her proper value'. Charles Dickens's daughter described her, in later life, as 'a woman of great wit and humour – but a devil!'. Kate Dickens was known for her somewhat acerbic asides – she once described Wilkie as being 'as bad as he could be' for keeping a mistress – and may have meant no more than that Harriet Collins was occasionally cutting or caustic in conversation.

In the second year of Collins's life the family spent the summer and autumn in a cottage in Hendon; soon after their return, in the spring of 1826, they moved from New Cavendish Street to Pond Street by Hampstead Green. Theirs was the second house in a row of small houses running down a hill, in a spot now covered by the Royal Free Hospital. Hampstead became for Collins another sacred spot. It is of course the setting for the first appearance of the woman in white, at the junction of Finchley Road with West End Lane and Frognal Lane, and was in Collins's childhood a village among the fields. His father was therefore, according to Collins, 'surrounded by some of the prettiest and most varied inland scenery that this part of England presents'. The family was enlarged here by the birth of Charles Allston Collins, at the beginning of 1828.

In his own account the childhood of Wilkie Collins was an unexceptionable if happy one. 'Tell Willy,' his father wrote, 'I have this day picked up two nice little scuttle-fish bones for him.' William Collins sketched his infant son, showing his nervous and delicate features with the slight protuberance above his temple. The novelist remembered sitting on the knee of his godfather, Sir David Wilkie, and watching him draw cats and dogs and horses. He went skating with his younger brother, and averaged thirty tumbles on each outing.

There were the usual family holidays. In the summer of 1829 they travelled to Boulogne for six weeks, in the hope that a change of air might restore the health of his ailing grandmother. They rented a house in the marketplace, from the window of which William Collins sketched the more picturesque aspects of French peasant life. It was here that the young boy was told one of those melodramatic stories that made such an impression upon his imagination. Years later he remembered how a Boulogne fisherman had rescued a black seaman from a shipwreck; the mariner was refused admission to any house, as a result of the restrictions of quarantine, and so the fisherman lay alongside the man all night 'endeavouring to restore the dying negro by the vital warmth of his own body'. His efforts, unhappily, did not succeed.

In the early autumn of the year the Collins family migrated to Ramsgate, a resort to which Wilkie returned throughout his life. In his early years there was really nothing there except the sea, but the sea haunted Collins like a passion; in the dusty streets of London he longed for it and scarcely a year passed without a visit to Broadstairs or Ramsgate – or even further afield, to Cornwall or the Isle of Man.

They had moved to a larger house in Hampstead Square but then a year later, in 1830, they made the journey south to Bayswater. The house in Porchester Terrace lay at a distance from 'the Oven' or 'the Great Wen', as London was known, but it was not immune from the agitation of the larger world. Collins remembered the demonstrations of 1832 surrounding the passage of the great Reform Bill. 'My poor father', he wrote, 'was informed that he would have his windows broken if he failed to illuminate'; that is, he was obliged to put a lamp or candle in every window. The two boys were 'mad with delight', and saw the demonstrators 'marching six abreast (the people were in earnest in those days) provided with stones'. William Collins himself was a high Tory, and did not look with favour upon such celebrations. He may have been the inspiration for a dinner party in *The Moonstone* when one of the company 'growing hot at cheese and salad time, about the spread of democracy in England, burst out as follows: "If we once lose our ancient safeguards, I beg to ask you, what have we got left?" . . .'

William Collins also had more private complaints. In the summer of 1833 he reported to his wife, from the country house of a patron, that 'my nerves are stronger and the pain in my face is fast decreasing'. He wrote in his diary that 'I am sadly low in mind at times, and in body weak'. It is tempting to see the laws of heredity in operation. Both Wilkie and Charles Collins suffered from 'nerves' and Wilkie, in particular, was plagued by pains in his face and eyes. Mrs Collins was also treated for 'nerves' in Brighton. This was an age of anxiety and in one of his novels Collins described 'these days of insidious nervous exhaustion and subtly-spreading nervous malady'. Far from being the boisterous and confident masters of empire, the Victorians were prey to nervous derangement as a consequence of what they called 'the battle of life'.

At the beginning of 1835, at the age of eleven, Wilkie Collins was enrolled at the Maida Hill Academy, a day school just off the Edgware Road. He seems to have been a model pupil because, at the end of his first year, he won as first prize in class a two-volume set of Southey's *Essays*. He kept the books in his library for the rest of his life. In the schoolboy community, however, success is not necessarily applauded. In an essay he wrote that 'the idle boys deserted him as a traitor, the workers regarded him as a rival; and the previous winner gave him a thrashing'. Wilkie Colllins did not like school.

He was also finding out for himself the joys of private reading. He devoured his mother's collection of Gothic romances while discovering such staples of childhood as *The Arabian Nights*, *Robin Hood* and *Don Quixote*. He worshipped Walter Scott and admired Byron. It might plausibly be suggested that he always preferred 'light' reading; he was by no means a scholar or an intellectual, and preferred adventure to analysis.

On his frequent trips away from home William Collins tried to supervise his sons' moral education. 'Tell the dear children', he instructed his wife, 'that the only way they can serve their parents is to obey them in all things: let Charley find out the passages in Scripture where this duty is most strongly insisted on, and write them down for me.' He urged the boys themselves to 'go on praying to God, through Jesus Christ, to enable you, by his Holy Spirit, to be blessings to your parents'.

These moral admonitions may have meant very little to Wilkie Collins. In later life he scorned pious sentiment. '*You* keep on cramming church down his throat,' the father of one six-year-old boy is told in *Hide and Seek*, 'and *he* keeps puking on it as if it was physic . . . Is that the way to make him take kindly to religious teaching?'

Yet the father's sense of religious obligation does not seem to have curtailed the social life of his family. He of course knew many of the eminent artists of the period, but his acquaintance stretched to the more interesting poets. Samuel Taylor Coleridge, for example, seems to have struck up a friendship with Mrs Collins. Wilkie once recalled to a friend an occasion when the poet broke down in tears while describing to her his addiction to opium. 'Mr

Coleridge, do not cry,' he remembered her as saying, 'if the opium really does you any good, and you must have it, why do you not go and get it?' Since Wilkie was himself at this time addicted to laudanum, his precocious memory may have had something to do with self-justification.

In this childhood period Wilkie, by his own account, seems to have suffered from the afflictions of first love. She was the wife of one of his neighbours, three times his age. He was so obsessed by her that he took a violent dislike to her husband and ran away whenever he encountered him. He could not of course take a 'liberty' with her, and so he suffered in silence. His susceptibility to women is obvious throughout his life, and he seems to have been in love with half of his female acquaintance. He needed the society of women and, with two mistresses to keep him company for much of his life, he clearly needed more intimate attentions. He told his friends, in later life, that his sexual initiation came under a foreign sky.

3

The Pilgrimage

At nine o'clock on the morning of Monday 19 September 1836, the Collins family took a 'fly' to Piccadilly where they picked up the Dover coach. They were on their way to Italy. The journey had long been discussed. Sir David Wilkie had suggested to William Collins that a study of the Italian masters would prove invaluable to his own art. Collins hesitated, unwilling to break off his sons' education at a sensitive stage, but Sir David Wilkie and other friends persuaded him that the boys would gain more profit from the experience than in the study of schoolbooks. And so it proved. Wilkie Collins, twenty-five years later, said that he had learned more in Italy 'which has since been of use to me, among the pictures, the scenery and the people, than ever I learnt at school'. Italy was the dream of the hard-pressed, weary and anxious Victorians. It was the home of sensation and of ease, of colour and of sunlight; it represented soul and spirit rather than money and materialism.

The Collins family took the steamboat from Dover to Boulogne; four days later they arrived in Paris. His parents did not care for the city; they did not like the smells and, according to Mrs Collins, there were 'no shops to be compared to Regent Street'. Wilkie loved it. In later life it became his city of choice; he admired the scenic pageant of the boulevards and the vivacity of the people. Mrs Collins disliked the food also – 'tough mutton', she wrote, 'but glad of anything plain'. Her son, in contrast, became something of a gourmand.

They made their slow way south towards the Mediterranean.

Martigues, just beyond Arles, was 'furnished with one small inn, the master of which, never having seen an Englishman before, sat down to dinner with his customers, and kept his cap on with edifying independence'. So Wilkie wrote in his memoir of his father. They travelled on to Marseilles, which according to Mrs Collins 'smelled in a disgusting manner'. It was soon time to move on to Cannes and to Nice, where they remained for six weeks.

Italy beckoned just beyond the frontier. In the middle of December they hired a carriage to Genoa, William Collins leaning out of the window in order to sketch 'the wild torrents – the mighty precipices – the cloud-topped mountains' that they passed along the Cornice road. His father said that the scenery 'nearly drove him mad'. A steamship took them to Livorno, from where they proceeded to Florence. A journey by way of Siena and the Apennines brought them to Rome, where William Collins believed that he had reached 'the shrine of his pilgrimage'. The family stayed here until the spring. They found lodgings in the Via Felice, where in a niche a Madonna rose above cabbage stalks and general rubbish. William Collins settled to some serious painting, in a borrowed studio, but even from the window of his apartment he was enchanted by what he saw of the Romans 'in their carelessness of repose, in their unconscious sublimity of action, in their natural graces of line and composition'. Wilkie took up Italian lessons.

The family saw everything. They visited the Vatican and the Sistine Chapel; they went to the horse races; they admired the Colosseum, 'doubly mysterious and sublime in the dim, fading light'; they attended the opera and the ballet; they watched all the ceremonies of Holy Week, with the two boys racing to St Peter's to see the washing of the pilgrims' feet; they sauntered on the Pincian Hill, which became the setting for Collins's first published novel, *Antonina*. 'Who', he wrote, 'after toiling through the wonders of the dark, melancholy city has not been revived by a visit to its shady walks and by breathing its fragrant breezes?'

He came to reminisce, too, about 'the magnificent Roman women of the people . . . gossiping and nursing their children' in the streets. One woman, in particular, caught his eye. Charles Dickens repeated the story in a letter to his sister-in-law. He said that Collins 'gave us . . . in a carriage one day, a full account of his first love adventure. It was at Rome it seemed, and proceeded, if I may be allowed the expression, to the utmost extremities – he came out quite a pagan Jupiter in the business.' He may have been exaggerating, in a fit of male bravura, but it is perfectly possible that a thirteen-year-old boy could seduce or be seduced by an older woman.

It may be surmised, in fact, that Wilkie was becoming something of a voluptuary or at least a young man whose sexual awareness was awakened early. 'I think the back view of a finely formed woman the loveliest view,' he wrote at the age of sixty-three, 'and her hips the most precious parts of that view.' He dwells with loving care on the descriptions of his female characters, so that the figure of one of them is 'slender, but already well developed in its slenderness, and exquisitely supple'. When the American photographer Sarony sent him a selection of female nudes he pored over them, and particularly admired a 'Venus' about to enter her bath; he framed it and placed it on his desk. In *Antonina* Vetranio, a wealthy Roman, asks his slave merchants to send him the most beautiful women in the empire so that they can be displayed before him 'of every shade in complexion and of every peculiarity in form'. It is not hard to see the predilection of the author as well as the lust of the character.

He mentioned to Sarony that his ideal was the 'Venus Callipygian', a statue that he may have seen in the National Museum of Naples on the next stage of the Italian tour. It is the back view of a woman with very prominent shapely buttocks, and Collins told the photographer that 'my life has been passed in trying to find a living woman who is like her – and in never succeeding'. So, perhaps, he was always in pursuit of the ideal fantasy. This may account for the evident fact that in his fiction the women are rarely as physically vivid as the men; the females are often idealised rather than described, whereas the males come alive with a sudden concrete or striking detail. His fondness for women may have impeded his muse.

From Rome, at the beginning of May, the Collins family travelled to Naples. For three weeks William Collins sketched the bay and the coastline, together with the fishing-craft and the fishermen; he also found fresh material in 'the great army of vagabonds, male and female, eating, drinking and sleeping in the streets'. He was about to embark on more extensive projects, when the family began to notice 'strange-looking yellow sedan chairs, with closed windows' passing in the streets; the passengers had all been stricken with cholera. The fear of quarantine was now upon the family.

So they repaired at some speed to Sorrento on the other side of the bay. It ought to have been an ideal retreat but the heat of the southern Italian summer may have affected them. In her diary Mrs Collins professed to be 'quite overcome' and then noted that 'Willy very tiresome all day. His father obliged to punish him at dinner-time. Made us all miserable.' The boy then locked his mother on the roof; whether by accident, or design, is not clear. Collins himself now fell ill with rheumatism and inflammation of the eyes, complaints which would one day cripple his son. Camphor and castor oil did not ease his suffering, and the sulphur baths of Ischia were recommended.

So the family set sail to the little island. Collins began to recover here, but his oldest son was in ill humour. 'Willy in disgrace again.' When they returned to Naples, at the lifting of the epidemic, Charles Collins managed to break his arm. It would seem now that the Italian adventure was over. In early February they left Naples and returned to Rome. From there it was a leisurely progress towards home, taking in Venice, Bologna, Parma, Verona and Padua on the way. The final journey took them down the Rhone to Cologne and Rotterdam. When they arrived in London on 15 August 1838, they had been away for almost two years.

There is no doubt that the young Wilkie Collins was thoroughly changed by the experience. His natural education had been advanced and, unlike most young men of his position, he had observed and lived in a society quite different from that of middle-class England. He had learned to read French and to gabble in Italian. He may also have been fortunate enough to have had his first sexual experience. He felt himself to be different.

Yet once more he was obliged to endure the company of London schoolboys. On the family's return they moved to a house in familiar territory close to Regent's Park, 20 Avenue Road, and Collins was soon despatched to a boarding school in the northern region of Highbury. Henry Cole's Academy, overlooking Highbury Fields, was not a public school in the grand manner, but it was respectable and relatively inexpensive at £90 per year. The Reverend Cole was also minister of the Providence Chapel in Islington.

Wilkie was still close to home, and does not seem to have suffered the martyrdoms that have afflicted other sensitive English schoolboys. The prefect in his dormitory, however, seems to have been something of a tyrant. According to Wilkie he 'was as fond of hearing stories when he had retired for the night as the Oriental despot to whose literary tastes we are indebted for The Arabian Nights'. He would tell the hapless schoolboy that 'you will go to sleep, Collins, when you have told me a story'. If Wilkie did well, he was given a pastry; if he failed to entertain he felt the cat-o'-nine-tails. This itself is a good story, and may have been embellished in the telling, but it suggests that his characteristic gift was appreciated. Wilkie already had some skill at reading aloud. He recited passages from Mary Shelley's *Frankenstein* and Matthew Lewis's *The Monk* to his aunt and her assorted guests, from whom the response was 'Lord!', 'Oh!', 'Ah!' and 'Good gracious!'. He liked to make the flesh creep. 'Your hair is uncommonly smooth at the present moment,' one of his characters says, 'but it will be all standing on end before I've done.'

Wilkie had other memories of the academy. He seems to have acquired a reputation for idleness and inattention. 'If it had been Collins,' he recalled one master as saying, 'I should not have felt shocked and surprised. Nobody *expects* anything of *him*. But You!! – etcetera etcetera.' The fact that he had mastered the elements of French, evident in his lessons, probably marked him as an outsider. He was more worldly wise, and more travelled, than any of his contemporaries. Two of his letters from school to his mother are in Italian, written less as an exercise than as a cipher to evade the prying eyes of his masters. In that language he calls the academy 'the prison' and 'this cursed place'. It is clear enough that he did not believe he belonged there. His general oddity, or eccentricity, would not in any case have recommended itself to average English boys.

Compensations could be found. His mother sent him cake, which he described as 'delectably luscious'. In winter he was able to slide on the frozen ponds of the vicinity. One boy swallowed spiders for a penny. Wilkie also reassured his mother that his eyes were better, which suggests something of the inflammation that would cause him agonies at a later date. It must have been a relief, however, to leave behind his schooldays at the age of sixteen. No more Latin. No more Greek. Yet what was to be done with him? William Collins considered the possibility of his son's taking holy orders. 'My father', Wilkie wrote, 'proposed sending me to the University of Oxford, with a view of my entering the Church.' On reflection, however, it was clear that he was wholly unsuited to the ministry. He was naturally averse to respectability in any of its forms. He was always ready to disparage the 'clap-trap morality' of the nineteenth century. The student allowance, necessary for keeping up appearances, may also have been too large for William Collins's pocket. Wilkie told his father that 'I thought I should like to write books', but this was considered to be a wayward youthful enthusiasm that would lead to a life of poverty in a garret. In the absence of a viable alternative, therefore, the seventeen-year-old was consigned to a career in commerce.

The health of William Collins had not improved since the maladies of Sorrento, and it was believed by his doctor that his rheumatism was exacerbated by the fact that the house in Avenue Road lay on damp clay soil. So in the summer of 1840 the family migrated to the drier region of Oxford Terrace, a little to the north of Hyde Park. It was from here that Wilkie Collins walked every morning, or took the omnibus, to the offices of Antrobus & Company at the west end of the Strand close to Trafalgar Square.

He was now apprentice to a firm of tea importers. Since Edmund Antrobus was a friend of William Collins, it is likely that he was granting the painter a favour by taking on his son as an unpaid apprentice rather than as a salaried clerk. In this way Wilkie would get 'to know the business' and accustom himself to the methods of commerce. It was also a means of keeping him occupied. Idleness was a sin.

So Wilkie suffered on an office stool, where he copied invoices and bills of lading. In one of his novels, *Hide and Seek*, another young man enters the office of a tea broker and, after three weeks of employment, voices his complaint. 'They all say it's a good opening for me, and talk about the respectability of commercial pursuits. I don't want to be respectable, and I hate commercial pursuits.' That may be deemed to be the authentic voice of Wilkie Collins. 'Only fancy me going round tea-warehouses in filthy Jewish places like St Mary-Axe, to take samples, with a blue bag to carry them about in; and a dirty junior clerk, who cleans his pen in his hair, to teach me how to fold up parcels!'

Wilkie may have expressed his displeasure to his father since, in the spring of 1842, William Collins wrote to one of his patrons, Sir Robert Peel, with a request that his son might be granted entry to the Civil Service. Peel was then the First Lord of the Treasury, in which department his son 'might have the prospect, however distant, of rising to eminence'. Peel was discouraging. Wilkie remained with Antrobus & Company for a further four years. He seems to have done his work quickly and then to have devoted his time to scribbling poems, plays, stories, anything. He admitted later that he had produced vast quantities of nonsense, and yet it was the necessary preparation for the career he would eventually follow. There may have been times when he was frustrated and morose.

In the summer of 1842, however, William Collins took his son on a painting tour of Scotland. They travelled by sea to Edinburgh, where he visited the Old Town and climbed Arthur's Seat; then they journeyed on by steamer to Wick, in the north of Scotland, before going on to Lerwick in the Shetlands. Collins had been asked to furnish illustrations for Sir Walter Scott's *The Pirate* set in this wild and desolate landscape. Wilkie himself invoked it in later novels, with the moorland and the bog and the dripping white mist. On one occasion he and his father were lost on the moor, and were told to 'leave it to the pownies'.

In his memoir of his father he recalls the 'small dull glow of light lingering in the western hemisphere' and 'the bright, pure northern twilight which streamed through their bedroom windows at *midnight*'. He describes 'Mr Collins, with one knee on the ground, steadying himself against the wind; his companion [Wilkie Collins] holding a tattered umbrella over him, to keep the rain off his sketch book'. In the memoir, also, he interprets his father's painting in vibrant terms, and these short prose pieces convey Wilkie's interest in painterly composition. Of one landscape he wrote that 'the sky is tinged by a mild, dawning light, which arises over a bank of misty vapour, and touches the wild, sharp edges of a large cloud'.

He possessed a painter's eye, and learned much from his intimacy with his father's work. He learned how in narrative terms to set off mass and detail on his canvas, and how to fix the proportions of light and shade or comedy and pathos. On the preparation for his novels he told one correspondent that 'all this is done, as my father used to paint his skies in his famous sea-pieces, at one heat'. When he explained that William Collins fashioned an art which 'connected the figures with the landscape, making each of equal importance' he was also describing his own practice. Thus, in *The Moonstone*, 'I saw the raging sea, and the rollers tumbling in on the sand-bank, and the driven rain sweeping over the waters like a flying garment, and the yellow wilderness of the beach with one solitary black figure standing on it – the figure of Sergeant Cuff.' His novels resemble a series of pictures rather than a sequence of scenes. Yet the innate sympathy between character and landscape, in all of his work, means that the pictures are animated by dramatic life. In small as well as large matters the metaphors of the painter's trade came naturally to him. On completing *The Woman in White* he wrote to a friend that 'I have done! (except for my *varnishing days* in respect of proof sheets)'; a 'varnishing day' was the day before the exhibition at the Royal Academy when the artists could apply their finishing touches.

Then, after the wilderness of the Shetlands, he and his father returned to the desolation of London. The family moved once more; they travelled only a short distance and decamped round the corner to Devonport Street. This house had the great advantage of containing a room that could be employed as a studio, the first William Collins had ever possessed. Wilkie described just such a studio in one of his novels, with its pots and brushes, scraping knives, chalks and pencils, rags smeared with paint and oil. He also referred to a very special trick of his father, who had painted a quill pen and sable brush upon the floor; they were so exactly reproduced that visitors would stoop to pick them up, at which point William Collins would invariably laugh at his successful practical joke.

Wilkie returned to his office stool at Antrobus & Company, but now there was a significant difference in his life. He was about to become an apprentice in quite another sense. In 1843, at the age of nineteen, he became a published writer.

4

First Light

The offices of Edmund Antrobus were situated in one of the centres of the London publishing world. Chapman & Hall, which had already published *The Pickwick Papers* and *Nicholas Nickleby*, was close by; the offices of *Punch*, the *Illuminated Magazine* and the *Illustrated London News* were in the vicinity. Wilkie may already have started writing reviews but, since they were anonymous, any such pieces have long ago been lost.

His first work is a slight piece of rodomontade entitled 'Volpurno'; its existence is only known because it was reprinted in a New York journal, and its first English publication is not recorded. It is a Poe-like story, set in Venice, of doomed love between a beautiful Englishwoman and a demented student of astronomy. It is of no real interest, except as an indication of Collins's tendency towards sentimentality and Gothic melodrama. In the summer of 1843 he published one of his first sketches, 'The Last Stage Coachman', in the *Illuminated Magazine*. The dominant influence here is that of Dickens rather than Poe, and it is a lament on the replacement of the stagecoach by the railway train. 'We wasn't full but we wasn't empty,' the eponymous coachman says, 'we wos game to the last!'

This was written at the peak of what became known as 'railway mania', and is an indication that Wilkie began his writing career at a time when social and economic change was all around him. The look of the coachman, at an arriving train, was 'the concentrated essence of the fierce and deadly enmity of all the stage coachmen of England to steam conveyance'. He was looking at the network of rails that now covered much of England with 5,000 miles of line, at the factories growing larger and more efficient, at the rapid development of the cities and the industrial towns, at the growth of the suburbs, at the increase of population, at the radical changes in agricultural practice, at what Charles Dickens describes in *Dombey and Son* as 'competition, competition – new invention, new invention – alteration, alteration'.

He must have showed his first published pieces with some pride to his father, who in the following year submitted them to the President of Corpus Christi for his literary opinion. He reported to his wife that 'Dr Norris . . . thinks he ought to do great things.' Collins himself was sufficiently impressed to confide to his diary that 'I think it quite possible that my dear son, William Wilkie Collins, may be tempted, should it please God to spare his life beyond that of his father, to furnish the world with a memoir of my life.'

Wilkie was willing enough to throw himself into any literary enterprise, and in 1843 began work on his first novel. *Ioláni* was set in Tahiti where 'my youthful imagination', as he wrote later, 'ran riot among the noble savages'. For the nineteen-year-old, Tahiti was also delectable because of its association with free love. He was already a fantasist. Yet he did his homework, too, and consulted the four volumes of William Ellis's *Polynesian Researches* as well as Basil Hall's *Fragments of Voyages and Travels*; throughout his life he was inspired by documentary material, and in the process he breathed upon facts and kindled them into life.

In the summer of 1844 he broke off his labours, both in the study and in the office, to travel to Paris with Charles Ward. Ward was courting Wilkie's cousin and, although he was ten years older than Collins, they made good travelling companions. In later life, having joined Coutts & Company, he became the writer's financial adviser. Yet now they were young, and they were in Paris. They were abroad for five weeks, suggesting that the terms of

Wilkie's apprenticeship were not strict ones. They intended to follow the early stages of the route of Yorick in Laurence Sterne's *A Sentimental Journey*, but their true destination was the capital of dissipation. Just before leaving Collins had also purchased the works of François Rabelais, hitting the right bawdy and sybaritic note before a journey to the Continent.

His letters from Paris to his mother record his visits to the gardens, the theatres, the cafés and the opera houses; there was no end of eating and drinking, confirming that Wilkie was already an aficionado of French food which he extolled all his life. He also wanted to know whether Antrobus would extend his leave of absence. He signed his letters 'Wilkie Collins', rather than 'Willie' or 'Willy', as a mark of the independence he now felt to be his due. His father was not impressed by his Parisian high spirits. 'I do not like his flippant companion,' he wrote, 'they seem to think of nothing but doing absurd things.'

On his return Wilkie completed his composition of *Ioláni*. The plot, like most of Collins's plots, is perhaps too complex properly to summarise. Ioláni is a high priest, as evil as he is cruel, who fathers a child by the sentimental heroine Idía; he decides to sacrifice the child to his gods, in the ancient practice among the Tahitians of infanticide, but Idía flees into the verdant wilderness with a female companion named Aimáta. The machinations of the adventure included internecine warfare, wild men, and sorcery. The narrative is notable, however, for Collins's first depiction of abusive male power against women. It would become one of his principal themes. It is characteristic, too, that the two heroines are vigorous and spirited enough to fight back. Collins's later fiction is filled with independent females who defy the nineteenth-century stereotypes of femininity. *Ioláni* is an expressive, if languorous, fiction in the form of an intensely imagined reverie. Collins is an adult in craft, and an adolescent in sentiment. Murder and battle, funeral processions and wedding celebrations, are all seen in terms of theatrical spectacle; the chapters succeed one another in beautiful monotony, like waves crashing on the Tahitian shore.

He submitted the manuscript to the firm of Longman, which intimated that it might be willing to publish if Collins's father covered the costs of the enterprise; he then sent it to Chapman & Hall, who eventually declined to take it on. Other English publishers seem to have followed suit, and Collins put the pages away in a drawer. 'For the moment,' he wrote, 'I was a little discouraged. But I got over it and began another novel.' He now believed his future to be that of a writer.

He was also a young man about town. In the company of Charles Ward, and others, he was now able to explore the delights and dangers of London. He was still an apprentice in an office, of course, and no doubt followed the familiar life of the clerk at large in the streets of the city. It was a favourite theme for the essayists of the period. In *Hide and Seek*, while narrating the adventures of a young man in the tea trade, Collins dwells on the cheap delights of the town suffused 'with glitter and gas'; the chop-houses, the gin shops, the cookshops, the burlesque shows, all competed for attention. In the same novel he describes the poorer quarters where 'ballad-bellowing and organ-grinding and voices of costermongers' never cease their counterpoint to the general roar of London. Elsewhere Collins describes the street markets of the poor, with a detail that can only come from direct observation. Here were 'fish and vegetables; pottery and writing-paper; looking glasses, saucepans and coloured prints'. A vagabond sells apples from a donkey-cart, calling out, 'Who says the poor ain't looked after?' A blind man on the corner is selling boot laces and singing a psalm; an old soldier plays 'God Save the Queen' on a tin whistle, and a beggar wears a placard addressed to 'The Charitable Public'.

The cheap theatres were always an attraction. The performances, melodrama or pantomime according to taste, often did not finish until midnight. The air was foul, but the drink was plentiful. One penny was the price for admission; they were known as 'penny gaffs'. Aspiring actors paid for the privilege of taking on roles in Gothic horror, corrupted Shakespeare, sentimental comedy and domestic farce. It was the principal entertainment of the period before the advent of the music hall. The pit was filled with wooden backless benches, the audience as rough and as coarse as you would expect in the city. Dancing and singing often interrupted the proceedings on the stage with the women and children, according to Henry Mayhew, 'bringing an overpowering stench with them'. This is the other side of Victorian propriety and respectability, a contrast that Collins himself often noted.

Some night haunts opened when the theatres closed; they claimed to be places of 'musical entertainment', in which amateurs would sing to the accompaniment of a piano or a banjo. But essentially they were places of drink and dissipation. They reeked of brandy, bad breath and stale tobacco. The 'comic songs' were smutty and salacious. They were also the venue of the sisters of the streets in whom Wilkie had a profound interest. 'Are you good-natured, sir?' a prostitute remarks to a likely customer in one of his novels; it is a phrase that has the ring of authenticity. Wilkie often adverted to the plight of these women. As one contemporary wrote, 'hospitals do not as a rule admit them, dispensaries cannot cure them; even soup-kitchens for the sick will not help to feed them'.

When Charles Collins was admitted to the Royal Academy Schools, a further opportunity for more respectable celebration presented itself. Wilkie Collins drank so much on this occasion that he quoted the phrase from the Bible, 'my belly is as wine'. We may surmise that in these years, the young Wilkie was frequently inebriated. When he and his younger brother returned home at four in the morning, Charles Collins heard the cock crow and whispered that people out of doors that late 'were not in a fit state to die'. The younger Collins was in truth a diffident and nervous young man. He had an absolute horror of being left alone in the dark and his friend, Millais, bestowed on him the nickname of 'Old Timidity'.

Collins's father had never recovered his health, and from this time forward began sinking towards death. By the spring of 1844 he had contracted a persistent and wearing cough that left him weaker and weaker; after one particular bout of coughing, on attending a dinner party, he remarked that 'I have dined out for the last time.' He set out with his wife for the drier air of Anglesey, leaving the two boys at home. But the expedition did no permanent good; by the autumn of the year he was spitting blood. His nerves were very bad. The Collins household could not have been a happy one.

In the autumn of 1845, a few months after completing *Iolàni*, Wilkie decided to make the journey to Paris alone. He was now twenty-one and no doubt eager to claim and to assert his independence. He told his mother that on his crossing to Rouen, 'I made acquaintance with every soul in the ship, from a good hearted *negro* who told me he was a student in *philosophy*! To a man with a blood-spotted nose, who knew all the works, of all the artists, ancient and modern, all over the world.' Once installed in the Hôtel de Tuileries, on the rue de Rivoli, he began his life of unaccustomed freedom. He ate oysters and cutlets for breakfast, smoked cigars (a habit his father deplored) and drank innumerable cups of coffee. He was as always delighted by the more vivid scenes of ordinary life. The waiter in the hotel made strange cackling sounds of which 'omeberellaw' was one; it was a wet morning. Wilkie screamed with laughter at the noise he was making, and so did the waiter.

He was close enough to his mother to write her a stream of affectionate, if mildly sarcastic, letters. 'Give my love to the

Governor,' he wrote in one of them, 'and tell him that I will eat "plain food" (when I come back to England) and read Duncan's Logic and Butler's Analogy (when I have no chance of getting anything else to peruse).' Joseph Butler's *Analogy of Religion, Natural and Revealed* is a key work of Anglican apologetics. In a letter three days later Wilkie remarked that 'Mr Collins evinces a most unchurchmanlike disposition to scandalise other people'. Since Mrs Collins would have read these letters to her husband, it seems likely that they had a relaxed attitude towards their son's soft religious barbs.

He visited the Louvre and the Morgue, that depository of corpses lost and found which was a great favourite with English travellers. He bought opera glasses and visited the theatres; he purchased a box of soda powders so that he might indulge in feats of gastronomy. He bought some boots in the Parisian style and purchased a subscription with Galignani's Library, the English bookshop in Paris.

In the process he began to run out of money, and asked if his mother could raise £100 from Chapman & Hall on the strength of his manuscript of *Ioláni* which had not at this stage been rejected. 'You said you hoped I should make my Cheque last for my *trip*,' he told her. 'It *has* lasted for my *trip* but not for my *return*.' He was philosophical about the possibility of debtors' prison; it might even be preferable to imprisonment in the Strand, to which condition he was now obliged to return. The Paris adventure was, for the time being, over.

5

Triumph

On his return to London Wilkie Collins began serious work on what became his first published novel. *Antonina: or The Fall of Rome* is an historical romance set in Rome of the fifth century AD. He started writing it at night, in his father's studio, and all the evidence suggests that he approached his task carefully and professionally. After the failure of *Ioláni* to find a publisher, he wanted to ensure that the theme and the style of the new work were acceptable to a nineteenth-century audience. He was ready for a career as well as a vocation.

One of his principal sources was Edward Gibbon's *The History of the Decline and Fall of the Roman Empire* in which he read of the siege of Rome by 'the king of the barbarians', Alaric. As always he allowed his imagination to be stirred by documented facts, or at least by reputable sources. He acquired a pass for the Reading Room of the British Museum, where he could pursue his researches into the life of pagan Rome; in the first edition of the novel he listed his reading in footnotes and, in the preface, declared that he has sought 'the exact truth in respect to time, place and circumstance'.

Its immediate precursor is Bulwer-Lytton's *The Last Days of Pompeii*, an immensely successful novel published twelve years earlier; Collins was clearly eager to emulate that success, and his somewhat ornate and overwrought style is modelled on that of Lytton. The fashion for historical romances was in any case still in full flood. In 1837 G. P. R. James's *Attila* was published, followed two years later by William Ware's *Zenobia, or the Fall of Palmyra*.

But *Antonina* also draws also on his experience of Rome as a child. Once more he is back on the Pincian Hill which he had explored ten years before, where he had noticed the crack in the Aurelian Wall that plays so large a part in the plot; he walks again in imagination through the picturesque, if malodorous, passages of the city.

Yet his historical fantasies were interrupted by present realities, when 'everybody seemed to conspire to shut the gates of the realms of fancy in my face'. A friend of William Collins proposed to him that his son should be called to the Bar, since barristers were eligible for many well-rewarded government appointments. Wilkie assented to the plan and, in the spring of 1846, he was enrolled as a student at Lincoln's Inn. He may have reflected that his great literary hero, Walter Scott, had also been called to the Bar and he may have believed that legal studies were not incompatible with literary achievement; he was soon disabused. He was introduced to the practice of conveyancing, and was obliged to study Blackstone's *Commentaries on the Laws of England*, dry fare after Gibbon and Bulwer-Lytton. 'I worked hard and conscientiously,' he wrote at a later date, 'but at the end of two months I had conceived such a disgust for the law that I was obliged to tell my father that I could endure the drudgery no longer.'

So instead he embarked on another continental journey. In the early summer he travelled to Belgium with Charles Ward, his companion in Paris two years before. This vacation lasted only for a week, in conditions of sweltering heat, and was comprised of little more than forays into Antwerp and Brussels and Bruges.

William Collins was perhaps displeased by his son's apparent disinclination for any of the professions, but by now his health was so broken down that he was in no position to intervene. He tried to continue work, but was often brought down by exhaustion and debility; he seems to have developed dropsy as well as an ailing heart. Wilkie wrote that 'his breathing was oppressed, as in the last stages of asthma . . . his cough assailed him with paroxysms'. William Collins took opiates, but they afforded only transitory relief. On 17 February 1847, in the company of his immediate family, he died.

Wilkie stopped work at once on *Antonina*, marking the place which he had reached on the night of his father's death; he noted in the manuscript that 'thus far I have written during my father's lifetime – this portion of chapter 3rd was composed on the last evening he was left alive'. Then, almost at once, he began planning his work upon *The Memoirs of the Life of William Collins R.A.* It was in a real sense a labour of love since Wilkie had a genuine respect and affection for his father. His mother furnished him with her own recollections and mentioned the names of friends and patrons to whom he might write for information. Within six weeks he had acquired most of the necessary material, and had advanced the narrative of his father's life to 1815.

He broke off in the summer of 1847 to visit France once more in the company of Charles Ward; his father had left the family financially independent, and so there was no need to seek out employment. Both young men were amateur artists, and had conceived a painting tour to take them through part of the French countryside. Four years later he would depict the journey in an essay for *Bentley's Magazine*, 'A Pictorial Tour to St George Bosherville', in which two young artists are driven to distraction by the heat and the gnats of Normandy. The narrator took with him a painting box stocked with a 'wonderfully complete assortment of colours, brushes, mill-boards, palette-knives, palettes, oil-bottles, gallipots, and rags' but not all the artistic tools in the world could favour the enterprise. The expedition was a disaster, and the narrator buried his botched painting in a shallow grave.

Collins and Ward did indeed leave Normandy after ten days, and of course migrated to Paris. He told his mother that 'we find provincial cities insupportably oppressive to our mercurial char-acters'; so Collins returned to the Hôtel de Tuileries on the rue de Rivoli. But Paris came at a price. Collins managed to over-spend, and asked his mother to send him a £5 note. The recently widowed mother may have decided to teach her son a lesson. No money arrived. Ward himself went back to London while Collins remained in Paris waiting for the 'needful'. A week passed without any relief in sight. In a state of some desperation, veiled by humour, he wrote to Ward asking him to forward £10; otherwise he would be obliged to pawn his watch and coat or take to the gaming tables to try his luck. By some means or other, he managed to cross the Channel.

He had told Ward that he was anxious to get back to his work on the *Memoirs*. But his attention was not entirely devoted to its composition. In the spring of the following year, for example, he was deep in a plot for the marriage of Ned Ward, Charles Ward's younger brother, to a much younger lady. This was the kind of scenario that he re-created in his fiction, and in which he seems to have been adept in life. Ned Ward, at the age of thirty-two, became engaged to Henrietta Ward, aged fourteen and a half; the coincidence of name was, in truth, coincidental. Her parents, naturally enough, were opposed to the marriage.

Wilkie Collins, hoping to ease the path of true love, opened his law books. He discovered that parental consent was required before a marriage could take place; nevertheless a false declaration did not impair the validity of a marriage. It simply rendered it illegal, leaving Ned Ward open to a period of imprisonment. The peculiar state of the marriage laws furnished much material for the novelist in later years. The two lovers obviously considered it worth the risk and, on 4 May 1848, were joined at All Souls' Church in Langham Place. Collins seems to have delighted in violating Victorian convention while, according to Henrietta, enjoining 'great caution and secrecy, as he planned out the whole affair with zest and enjoyment'. She added that he enjoyed 'the spice of romance and of mischief'.

After the ceremony the young bride returned to the house of her parents without saying a word. She had become part of what Collins once called, in a memorable phrase, 'the secret theatre of home'. Three months later she eloped with her husband for a honeymoon to Iver, near Slough; Wilkie had found rooms for them, and had seen them off in a cab. In recognition of his central role he became godfather to their first child. Mr and Mrs Ward relented, when faced with the fact of the marriage of their young daughter, and so all ended happily.

By the early summer of 1848 Collins had finished the life of his father and resumed work on his postponed novel, *Antonina*. He was also deep in negotiation with the publisher and engraver of the *Memoirs*; the firm of Longman was willing to take on the book, but only at the author's risk. Harriet Collins agreed to put up the money for the venture, thus honouring the husband while helping the son.

The Collins family moved once more to a smaller house, 38 Blandford Square, in Marylebone; the square is now no more than a sawn-off block of houses beside Marylebone Station, but in the 1840s it was part of a relatively new development. Collins was always acutely aware of the spread of London, with half-made gravel paths, scaffolding poles and boards and brick-kilns everywhere among patches and plots of waste ground.

Blandford Square becomes Baregrove Square in one of his novels, *Hide and Seek*; it is notable only for 'the dismal uniformity of line and substance in the perspective of the square'. In the rain and fog of a November morning the garden in the middle of the square is drab and dreary, with its close-cut turf and empty flower-beds and withered young trees 'rotting away in yellow mist and softly-steady rain'. The blinds of the brown brick houses are all drawn down, and the smoke from the chimney pots is lost in the fog. It is a perfect expression of a wet London winter.

Yet it was here that Mrs Collins entered a further and brighter phase of her existence; she became gregarious and vivacious, reclaiming some of the gaiety of her youth. She entertained her sons' friends, both artistic and literary, and acquired a reputation as a 'hostess'. Her sons themselves clearly adored her; Charles addressed her in his letters as 'my darling', and her death was the occasion for perhaps the greatest grief of Wilkie Collins's life.

Memoirs of the Life of William Collins R.A. was published by Longman, in November 1848; it was in two volumes and was dedicated to Sir Robert Peel, who had been one of William Collins's patrons. The son had paid his tribute to his father. In the process Collins had proved that he could master the long labour of composition and that he had an instinctive gift for narrative. It was published in an edition of 750 copies, and six weeks after publication, more than half of them were sold. Harriet Collins was no doubt happy, and relieved, when the book turned a small profit.

It is an agreeable and entertaining narrative, with just a hint of formal pedantry in its observations. But, for a young man of twenty-four, it is a formidable achievement with a judicious sorting of diaries, letters and biographic commentary to achieve a fully objective portrait of his father. Wilkie Collins himself does not intrude, except in the vigorous description of his father's painting; as Sir David Wilkie had said at his christening, he *sees*.

The reviews were excellent, further strengthening his sense of himself as a writer. The *Observer* said that 'no better work upon art and artists has been given to the world in the last half-century'. It was the best possible beginning for a professional novelist. On the title page the author inscribed himself as 'W.Wilkie Collins', which was itself an act of independence; he was no longer William, like his father. 'An author I was to be,' he wrote, 'and an author I became in 1848.'

In the summer of the following year the Collins household was thrown into disorder by a bout of amateur theatricals. These theatricals were a staple entertainment of the Victorian age; with no other diversions than the piano or the parlour game, these colourful and often costly productions offered all the pleasures of the theatre without any of the disadvantages of a 'low' audience. Great care was taken over the creation of a proper stage and over the provision of costumes and theatrical props. It was one of those communal and convivial activities for which the nineteenth century ought to be best remembered. Collins himself also seems to have enjoyed dressing up; at a 'Fancy Ball', a few months before, he had shaved off his whiskers and put on the wig, breeches and embroidered waistcoat of an eighteenth-century French rake.

The Good-Natur'd Man, a comedy by Oliver Goldsmith, is set in the same period. It was performed in the 'Theatre Royal, Back Drawing Room' of Blandford Square, and fourteen years later Collins looked back with nostalgia at the entertainment and excitement of a production in which he was actor as well as producer; he even wrote a verse prologue in the style of the eighteenth century. Ned Ward was part of the ensemble, as were some of Charles Collins's artistic acquaintance. They went on to act Sheridan's *The Rivals* in the same back drawing room.

Another actor in Goldsmith's comedy, Henrietta Ward, recalled that 'one day, just before the play was to be produced, the leading lady told Wilkie that she declined to act unless the leading gentleman was changed. Her reason was that he was "hideous".' The leading man then asked to resign on the grounds that the actress was an 'ogress'. Collins seems to be rehearsing these scenes in a novel of 1862. 'Private Theatricals!!!' a young woman announces in *No Name*. 'The Rivals is the play, papa – The Rivals by the famous what's his name – and they want ME to act!' This is only the prelude to 'the breaking of furniture and the staining of walls, to thumping, tumbling, hammering and screaming; to doors always banging, and to footsteps perpetually running up and down stairs'.

In the novel the actors frequently became hysterical, or fell ill at the wrong moment, or declined to act the part they had been given. 'Silence, gentlemen, if you please,' the actor-manager calls out, 'as loud as you like *on* the stage, but the audience mustn't hear you *off* it.' Stop. Toss your head. Pause. Look pertly at the audience. At the performance itself, 'a bursting of heated lamp-glasses, and a difficulty in drawing up the curtain'. Yet Wilkie Collins seems to have loved it all. These episodes presage his theatrical ventures of a later period.

In the cast of *The Good-Natur'd Man* were two young artists who soon enough would achieve great fame. William P. Frith and John Everett Millais, like Charles Collins, were associated with the Royal Academy and had been introduced to the rest of the Collins family. Millais himself had in the previous year established the 'Pre-Raphaelite' Brotherhood, at his parents' house in Gower Street, and its members were invited to evenings at Blandford Square. Harriet was the centre of attention, 'Jack' Millais was always asking her to 'fix the day' when they might be wed, and she struck up a lasting friendship with Holman-Hunt.

So we may imagine the circle of talented and even precocious young artists around Wilkie Collins. He was never entirely at ease with their work, but there is no doubt that he appreciated their company. All his life he had been surrounded by artists. He was himself once mistaken for a member of the 'PRB', and in 1850 Millais painted his portrait. The young Collins is portrayed in a reflective, even solemn mood; his small hands touch at the finger-tips suggesting contemplation of some difficult matter; his large grey eyes are partly hidden by a pair of spectacles; his mouth seems to be formed in a pout; he sports two rings, a large shirt-stud, and a watch chain.

Collins promised a magazine editor, at a later date, that he would 'do something amusing . . . about the Pre-Raphaelite Painting School in the country'; but he never did. Yet he gently mocks them in his genial portrait of a minor artist, Valentine Blythe, in *Hide and Seek*. He also seems to advert to them in a later novel, *The Black Robe*. 'Every little twig, on the smallest branch, is conscientiously painted – and the result is like a coloured photograph. You don't look at a landscape as a series of separate parts; you don't discover every twig on a tree; you see the whole in Nature, and you want to see the whole in a picture.'

Artistic success, of a kind, was also won by Wilkie Collins himself. In the Royal Academy's summer exhibition of 1849, a painting by Collins was accepted. *The Smugglers' Retreat* was displayed high up in the Octagon Room, close to the ceiling, in which disadvantageous position it failed to find a purchaser; Collins brought it home with him, and in later years it was hanging in his dining room. When he observed the much more accomplished artist, William Holman-Hunt, gazing at it he told him that 'you might well admire that masterpiece. It was done by that great painter Wilkie Collins, and it put him so completely at the head of landscape painters that he determined to retire from the profession in compassion for the rest.'

Even more welcome news soon followed when Richard Bentley, the publisher, decided to accept *Antonina*. Collins had written to him in the late summer of 1849, introducing himself and his book; he reassured Bentley that his research had been thorough and that he had taken pains to present it in a style that would be to the taste of the modern public. Secretly he was not confident of success, and had vague plans of publishing it himself.

Dickens had called Bentley 'the Burlington Street Brigand' on account of his high-handed dealings, but he seems to have dealt considerately with Collins. He read the first two volumes of *Antonina*, and liked what he saw. He was ready to come to an agreement. The young novelist had demanded £200. Bentley offered him £100 down, and a further £100 when the book had sold 500 copies. It was a fair enough arrangement, under the circumstances, and Bentley never had reason to regret his decision.

The novel was published at the end of February 1850, and it is clear from his letters that Collins was screwed up to the peak of excitement and expectation. He had already tried to arrange favourable reviews, from the magazines in which he had been published. He told Bentley that 'the proper letters have been written' to ensure favourable notice. He had no need to worry about its reception, however, and *Antonina* received more favourable reviews than any of its successors. Collins was even compared to Shakespeare. Certain reviewers warned the Victorian public about 'strong effects' and 'revolting details', but all were united in their praise. The *Morning Post* declared that the novel was sufficiently good to place its author 'in the very first rank of English novelists'. This, for a writer in his mid-twenties, was superlative praise. He also received congratulations closer to home. 'My mother', he wrote, 'thinks that I have written the most remarkable novel that ever was produced!' A second edition was published three months later.

Antonina would now be considered to be too highly pitched and melodramatic, but at the time it represented the familiar discourse of the historical romance in which lovely women and sinister men, sensitive souls and profligate wastrels, clean-limbed citizens and verminous soldiers, all strove for mastery. It has a dash of Walter Scott and a sprinkling of Bulwer-Lytton, combined with a very healthy respect for the tastes and predilections of the great public.

The novel is set at the time of Alaric's first siege of Rome and in a landscape of fear and threat the Romans and the Goths are portrayed as the opposite forces of humankind. Goisvintha, a harridan of ferocious temper, represents all the supposed fierceness of the Gothic female; unfortunately her brother, Hermanric, falls in love with a young Roman girl, Antonina. He finds her in the armed camp to which she has fled in fear of her father, Numerian, who is a grim-faced religious fanatic; meanwhile, back in Rome, the pagan Ulpius finds a crack in the Aurelian Wall through which he hopes to lead the Gothic forces. Long speeches are followed by lavish descriptions, all in the service of a melodrama driven by contrasts of character and of scene. Collins was always impressed by unfashionable moral loyalties and by parallel destinies. 'Here appeared a young girl, struggling half entombed in shields. There gasped an emaciated camp-follower, nearly suffocated in heaps of furs. The whole scene, with its background of great woods, drenched in a vapour of misty rain . . .' The narrator explains the whole effect as a 'gloomy conjunction of the menacing and the sublime', which is not an inappropriate description of the novel itself.

It is all sufficiently arresting to detain the reader, and there are marvellous passages of descriptive writing that culminate in a magnificently morbid Banquet of Famine and a vivid apocalyptic scene in a pagan temple reminiscent of the paintings of John Martin. Collins had told Bentley that he was anxious 'to make the *last* part of the story the *best* part'. In this, he succeeded. Yet *Antonina* is essentially hokum, crafted brilliantly by a young author already equipped with great technical powers. Unusually for a youthful novel, there is no oddity of style; there is no quirkiness or idiosyncrasy but, rather, that lucid and even tone that Collins never abandoned.

The novel also acquires a sober, and contemporary, flavour. London was even then being compared to imperial Rome, with premonitions of decay and dissolution. It was one of the great commonplaces of the period. Collins seems instinctively to sympathise with the poor and outcast of Rome. One of the Romans, unhappy with the enervated aristocrats who rule his city, calls out to the Goths 'with thousands who suffer the same tribulation that

I now undergo – "enter our gates! Level our palaces to the ground! Confound, if you will, in one common slaughter, we that are victims and those that are tyrants!"' Collins is entering a debate on the 'condition of England question', inaugurated six years before by Thomas Carlyle when he wrote that 'A feeling very generally exists that the condition and disposition of the Working Classes is a rather ominous matter at present.' It was a subject to which he would return.

Two days before the publication of *Antonina*, he had advanced a step further in the theatrical world. He translated a French melodrama and adapted it for the stage as *A Court Duel* at Miss Kelly's Theatre in Dean Street, Soho; the play, with Charles Collins in the lead, was performed at the end of February 1850 on behalf of the Female Emigration Fund, a charity that assisted poor women to settle in the colonies. It was Collins's first attempt at dramatic composition and his first exercise in the professional, or at least semi-professional, theatre. He always believed that he was, at heart, a dramatist.

6

Modern Times

The success of *Antonina* meant that Collins's literary career was assured. He was no longer the young man about town, living off his mother's income, but a young novelist with the London world before him. Yet he was also eager to extend the range of his writing. In the summer of the year, therefore, he embarked on a walking tour of Cornwall in search of the picturesque. His companion on this journey was a young artist from the Royal Academy, Henry Brandling, and their tour was meant to be practical rather than picaresque. Travelling books of a light-hearted nature, with text and illustration combined, were then fashionable; most parts of the British Isles had in fact been 'done', with the glaring exception of Cornwall. The county also had the attraction of being as yet beyond the ferocious maw of the railway network, and thus relatively unspoiled. The book was to be called *Rambles Beyond Railways*.

They reached the end of the line at Plymouth and then, with knapsacks on their backs, they took to the road. They were mistaken for pedlars and for 'mappers' in advance of the railway, which did in fact arrive a year later, but they received a cordial welcome from the natives who were not used to 'foreigners' in their neighbourhood. Collins was surprised and delighted by what he saw, and took copious notes. 'Rocks like pyramids – rocks like crouching lions . . . rocks pierced with mighty and measureless caverns.' Pilchards cost a penny per dozen. 'A distant, unearthly noise becomes faintly audible – a long, low mysterious moaning, that never changes, that is felt on the ear as well as heard by it . . .'

No one dies of starvation in Cornwall, although 5 per cent of the population of the Penzance area have migrated to New Zealand or Australia. 'Far out on the ocean the waters flash into a streak of fire.' The people of Looe once cleared a plague of rats by cooking and eating them with onions.

Collins himself appears in the familiar role of the hapless traveller, a small man in a large county. When he descended into a copper mine at Botallack, their guide inspected him. 'Only let me lift you about as I like,' he said, 'and you shan't come to any harm.'

Collins wrote the book in his study at 17 Hanover Terrace, the house on the fringe of Regent's Park to which Harriet Collins had moved in his absence. This was to be his home for the next six years, a large and commodious dwelling in what was considered to be healthy air. Its size can be deduced from the fact that, in 1852, the family gave a dance for seventy guests. It was here that the Collins family held numerous dinner parties. 'Nothing could well exceed the jollity of those little dinners,' Holman-Hunt recalled. 'In any case Mrs Collins did not often make our smoking after the meal a reason for her absence from our company. We were all hard-worked people enjoying one another's society and we talked only as such can.' Millais himself treated Hanover Terrace as his second home. It was to this house, too, that Collins invited the most famous novelist in the world.

He had met Charles Dickens in the spring of 1851. They had come together over their shared passion for amateur theatricals, when in this year Dickens decided to perform a comedy by Bulwer-Lytton, *Not So Bad As We Seem*, for the sake of a literary charity. Dickens had known William Collins, and now was happy for the opportunity to enlist the services of the son. 'I think *you* told *me* that Mr Wilkie Collins would be glad to play any part in Bulwer's Comedy,' he wrote to a mutual friend, Augustus Egg, 'and I think *I* told *you* that I considered him a very desirable recruit.' Dickens was to be the star of the drama, and Collins was to play the part of his valet.

Dickens and Collins met at the house of John Forster, later to become Dickens's biographer, in Lincoln's Inn Fields. Dickens was some twelve years older than Collins but they amused or impressed each other; soon enough, they had become firm friends. Dickens's 'young men' were an assorted bunch of young journalists and aspiring writers who worshipped at the shrine of 'the Inimitable', but from the beginning Collins seems to have held a higher place in the older novelist's affections. They explored London together, in search of the quaint or the queer; they attended the theatre, dined at good restaurants and collaborated both on stories and on plays. Collins was already an habitué of London night life, with all of its social and sexual possibilities, and there is little doubt that Dickens enjoyed the company of his genial and unconventional partner on what he called their 'Haroun Alraschid' excursions to dance halls and other places of entertainment. Alraschid was of course the protagonist of *One Thousand and One Nights*, the caliph of Baghdad who slept with a different virgin every night.

It was first agreed that *Not So Bad As We Seem* should be played at the London home of the Duke of Devonshire, Devonshire House. The audience was to include Victoria and other members of the royal family; it was, in other words, to be in every sense a glittering occasion. Dickens rehearsed his cast, in his usual relentless fashion, two nights a week for five hours at a time. The first performance was given in the middle of May, 1851, in front of the Queen and the Prince Consort as well as the Duke of Wellington. Victoria noted in her diary that 'all acted on the whole well'. Dickens told his wife that 'Collins was *admirable* – got up excellently, played thoroughly well, and missed nothing'. The play was very much in demand; further performances were given in the Hanover Square Rooms and, towards the end of the year, a provincial tour was organised in which Collins still played his part.

On its publication by Richard Bentley at the beginning of 1851 the narrative of Collins's Cornish adventures, *Rambles Beyond Railways: Or Notes in Cornwall taken a-foot*, proved to be a success, with a second edition published two years later. Collins, however, was still eager to write for the public prints. 'The Twin Sisters' appeared in *Bentley's Miscellany*, a short story only notable for being his first exercise in contemporary melodrama; it was the genre in which he would excel. He was also writing essays and reviews for the *Leader*, a weekly newspaper of radical persuasion; he owed the connection to a fellow student at Lincoln's Inn, Edward Pigott, who had become its editor.

His first signed essay, 'A Plea for Sunday Reform', was essentially an attack upon the Sabbatarian views of his father; it was an eloquent request that the lot of the working classes could be ameliorated if places of innocent entertainment were allowed to open on Sunday. Museums might therefore be preferred to public houses. 'You set the church doors open and tell him to go in,' he wrote. 'If he turns away, you abandon him to the gin palaces at once.' Collins also wrote book reviews and dramatic notices for the magazine, and maintained his connection with it for several years.

The fact that Collins wrote for a radical magazine has often been suggested as a clue to his politics, if in fact he had any politics. He was essentially liberal in his social and political views, averse to coercion and conflict; he showed some sympathy with the principles of socialism as it was then understood, and was instinctively on the side of the oppressed. As he wrote in *The Fallen Leaves* (1879), these were 'the people who have toiled hard after happiness and have gathered nothing but disappointment and sorrow; the friendless and the lonely, the wounded and the lost'. In the same novel the principal character rails against 'those organized systems of imposture, masquerading under the disguise of banks and companies', with the exploitation of cheap labour 'regarded, on the highest commercial authority, as "forms of competition" and justifiable proceedings in trade'. Yet it remains very doubtful whether Collins had a coherent political philosophy, being in most respects a conventionally Victorian freethinker. 'I hate controversies on paper', he told Pigott, 'almost more than I hate controversies in talk.'

Collins's religious views are almost as vague. He might best be described as a Christian humanist who accepted Christ as his Saviour but detested all formal and outward shows of religion. He preserved his particular wrath for evangelicals. He was neither an Anglican nor a Nonconformist; he was not Roman Catholic, and not an agnostic. In an age when unbelief was more common than is generally supposed, he was not an atheist. He rarely entered a church, and his actual beliefs are hard if not impossible to unravel. He is perhaps best described as an antinomian, happily contemplating diversity of opinion as well as a variety of churches. He may have believed with Charles II that God would not punish him for a few sins of pleasure.

He could now be considered a journalist as well as an author, and a stream of reviews and articles issued from his pen. Another of his stories, 'Mr Wray's Cash-Box', was published by Richard Bentley as a 'Christmas Book', a synthetic piece of seasonal comic fiction in the Dickensian manner; the reviewers liked it, but the public did not.

He may have decided that he was overworked, however, and certainly by the end of the year he needed the attentions of a doctor who forbade him to 'use' his brains at all. So he retreated to the country for 'a week of rest and restoration'. It was the beginning of a life that would come to be dominated by ill health and by the ministrations of the medical profession.

Bad health did not preclude him, however, from a lavish celebration in November after he had been called to the Bar. He had done no work for the past four years; he had simply attended the appropriate number of dinners in hall and paid the requisite fees. Nevertheless he decided to reward himself with what was known as a 'call-party'. 'What a night!' he wrote. 'What chicken! What songs! I carried away much claret . . . and am rather a seedy barrister this morning.' He never practised his new profession, and at a later date declared himself to be a barrister of fifteen years' standing without ever once receiving a brief or attending a courtroom. Yet the workings of the law play a vital part in most of his subsequent fiction. In eight of his novels, lawyers are prominent characters. They are part of his interest in plot and in detail, in the painstaking depiction of circumstance and in the melodramatic possibilities of wills and marriage settlements. 'I am a lawyer,' one of his characters reveals, 'and my business is to make a fuss about trifles.'

Even as he was touring in *Not So Bad As We Seem*, in the early months of 1852, Collins was deeply and energetically at work on his fiction. He published several stories, and prepared himself for his next novel. 'A Passage in the Life of Mr Perugino Potts' is an entertaining spoof on the life and ambition of an artist who bears a passing resemblance both to his father and to his brother. 'I may be wrong,' Potts writes, 'but my impression is that, as an Historical Painter, my biography will be written one of these days . . .' Collins also parodies the various styles that suggest themselves to a young artist in search of success.

He also wrote three stories of an occult or Gothic nature. 'Mad Monkton' dealt with the theme of inherited familial madness, and was found to be too disturbing for Dickens to publish in his weekly periodical, *Household Words*; it eventually found a home in *Fraser's Magazine*. 'A Terribly Strange Bed' did appear in *Household Words*, and reveals the workings of an ingenious instrument of suffocation and death in a Paris gambling den. It may owe something to Edgar Allan Poe; Poe had died three years before, but some of his short stories were not unknown to readers of the more lurid English periodicals. A copy of the 'Baudelaire edition' of Poe's collected works was also part of Collins's library. Collins, too, liked to make the flesh creep. 'Nine O'Clock!' is the story of fatality and clairvoyance that fits very well with the nineteenth-century fascination for mesmerism, hypnotism and spiritualism in all of its forms. Collins himself wrote a series of letters for the *Leader* on the subject, entitled 'Magnetic Evenings at Home'. He may have been attracted to the phenomena out of melodramatic, rather than scientific, interest.

Yet even when engaged in these fugitive pieces he was applying himself to his next novel. A very curious and interesting theme had occurred to him. What if a young man of breeding falls instantly in love with a young woman whom he sees on an omnibus? But what if that young woman is in all respects unworthy of him? What then? This is the story of *Basil*, a novel of fatality and obsession that might almost earn a place beside the great Russian novels of love and madness.

He began writing it at white heat, filling his square sheets with tiny handwriting, and it was concluded in the middle of September. He finished it while staying with the Dickens family in Dover, relaxing at the end of the gruelling dramatic tour in which the performers had been deafened by cheers and blinded by gas-light. The sea air acted on Collins as a restorative. The company of Dickens may have inspired his work on the sensational narrative; certainly Dickens's habit of sustained and professional composition offered Collins the best possible example. Dickens once told him that 'I was certain from the *Basil* days that you were the writer who would come ahead of all the field – being the only one who combined invention and power, both humorous and pathetic, and that profound conviction that nothing of worth is to be done without work.' Yet work was interrupted, at Dover, by long walks and by sea-bathing. One visitor to the Dickens household described Collins as 'a nice, funny little fellow but too much fond of eating and snuff'.

Basil: A Story of Modern Life was published by Richard Bentley in the middle of November 1852. The narrative of seduction and betrayal, of murderous violence and fatal infatuation, was strong meat for the Victorian public. In a long preface attached to the first version of the novel Collins declared that he was writing 'a story of our own times' and confessed that 'I founded the main event out of which this story springs, on a fact in real life which had come within my own knowledge.' The 'fact' concerns Basil's sudden infatuation with a young woman and his decision to marry her at all costs. It has been suggested that Collins was here recounting his own experience. Given his proclivities, this is possible. The only biographical sketch published in his lifetime, in part based on Collins's own reminiscences, alludes to an unhappy love affair.

Yet it is also possible that he was exaggerating the novel's realism as a way of making it seem 'new' and 'up to date'; he wanted to acquire as many readers as possible. There can be no doubt that he did genuinely wish to extend the frontiers of literary realism by taking account of 'the most ordinary street sounds that could be heard and the most ordinary street-events that could occur'. They become the setting for the drama, or the melodrama, of the narrative; Collins believed that 'the Novel and the Play are twin-sisters in the family of Fiction'. So the frantic action is played out against the background noise of 'the distant roll of carriages along the surrounding streets' and against the glow of the gas-lamps in the forlorn squares. It captures the theatre of modern life.

Basil follows the woman from the omnibus to one of those half-completed north London squares that Collins loathed; he soon discovers that Margaret Sherwin is the daughter of a linen-draper. This is the first shock. He is the scion of a noble family, and the difference in 'rank' is immense. Yet he perseveres and the linen-draper agrees to the marriage on the understanding that it is not consummated for a year; this will be time enough to placate Basil's father. Yet on the very night they were to become fully united Basil discovers that his bride has been carried off to a 'low' hotel (a brothel in the original version) by the linen-draper's confidential clerk, Robert Mannion. From an adjacent room he hears her seduction. '*I heard and I knew* – knew my degradation in all its infamy, knew my wrongs in all their nameless horror.'

This is the prelude to a narrative of revenge and suffering on a sensational scale. There is disfigurement; there is death; there is a violent climax in the wild scenery of Cornwall that Collins had recently visited. The obsessive relationship between Basil and Margaret Sherwin is pre-empted by the equally fatal association between Basil and Mannion. Collins seems to know well enough the nature of sexual jealousy and of jealous rage. Mannion himself is the archetype of Collins's later villains, smooth, hypocritical, pitiless; the natural malice of his nature is subdued by caution and patience, while his precise and deliberate speech conceals the turbulent passions that animate him. Only at one moment, illuminated by lightning, does he appear in his true form. 'It gave such a gloriously livid hue, such a spectral look of ghastliness and distortion to his features, that he absolutely seemed to be glaring and grinning on me like a fiend . . .' Although Collins was not at this stage dependent upon laudanum, he already evinces an addict's imagination.

It is true melodrama but melodrama of the highest kind in which a series of very intricate events and motives is effortlessly brought together. The plot, in the words of the narrative, 'shall ooze out through strange channels, in vague shapes, by tortuous intangible processes; ever changing in the manner of its exposure.' It is a spiritual, as well as a material, melodrama in which overwrought passion is finely conceived and conveyed. It conveys also the steady drumbeat of fate or, as Basil puts it, the 'superstitious conviction that my actions were governed by a fatality which no human foresight could alter or avoid'. *Basil* represents a very large advance in Collins's craft. It is a novel rather than a romance; it is written in the first person, a device that liberates his innately confessional mode; and it has been in part inspired by Dickens.

The critical reception was, to use a well-known word, mixed. The *Westminster Review* commented that the pivotal episode, in the seedy hotel, was 'absolutely disgusting'. This was a period in which the novelist was supposed to exhibit a 'high moral purpose'. The *Athenaeum* noted the 'vicious atmosphere in which the drama of the tale is enveloped' but also praised its 'gushing force'. The subtitle of the book, *A Story of Modern Life*, did not prevent one reviewer from criticising its pervasive air of unreality; Dickens himself noticed some improbabilities. In 1862 Collins stated that 'I knew that *Basil* had nothing to fear from pure-minded readers . . . Slowly and surely, my story forced its way through all adverse criticism, to a place in the public favour which it has never lost since.' Yet his real triumphs were still to come.

7

On the Road

Wilkie Collins, at the age of twenty-nine, was enjoying the fruits of his labours. He had a wide circle of friends; he attended Richard Bentley's literary dinner parties; he reviewed plays and books for the *Leader*; he had been introduced to the circle of writers and journalists around Dickens in the offices of *Household Words*; he became a member of at least three London clubs; he liked to dine out in the fashionable restaurants. And of course he invited artists and writers to Hanover Terrace; according to Holman-Hunt he was the most affable of hosts. Hunt wrote later that 'no one could be more jolly than he as the lord of the feast in his own house, where the dinner was prepared by a chef, the wines plentiful and the cigars of choicest brand. The talk became rollicking and the most sedate joined in the hilarity; laughter long and loud crossed from opposite ends of the room, and all went home brimful of good stories.'

He might be described as an eligible bachelor, except that he had no intention of marrying. He delighted in the companionship of women, and they enjoyed his company in return; one of those ladies, Eliza Chambers, said that to sit beside Collins at the dinner table was 'to have a brilliant time of it'. But he never once contemplated matrimony. He had already written in the memoir of his father that it was 'the most momentous risk in which any man can engage'. It was not a risk he cared to undertake, and instead he engaged in what might be described as two illicit relationships. In an article for *Household Words*, 'Bold Words by a Bachelor', he declared that 'the general idea of the scope and purpose of the institution of marriage is a miserably narrow one'; he did not intend, in other words, to bow to convention and propriety in the matter. He once ate a bride-cake, to be distributed to wedding guests, 'without the trouble of being married, or of knowing anybody in that ridiculous dilemma'. In his novels, too, he dilates upon the injustices and defects of the married state. It was one of his principal themes.

The pleasures of social life, however, were curtailed in the spring and early summer of 1853. He had completed almost half of a new novel, to be called *Hide and Seek*, when he was afflicted by an illness that may have anticipated the rheumatic gout or neuralgia of later years. Gout is associated with the pleasures of the flesh, but is often a genetic condition that provokes unusually large levels of uric acid in the blood; the acid crystallises in the joints, causing an acute form of arthritis with accompanying pain, stiffness and swelling. It may attack the hands and feet but, as in the case of Collins, the uric acid may accumulate around the eyes.

The fact that his father had suffered the same symptoms suggests that Collins may have inherited a predisposition to them, but anxiety and overwork may also have taken their toll upon his somewhat frail constitution. Whatever the diagnosis, he was in subsequent years often to be incapacitated by pain in the eyes and legs. He reflected on his experience in a later novel. 'The medical profession thrives on two incurable diseases in these modern days – a He-disease and a She-disease. She-disease – nervous depression. He-disease – suppressed gout. Remedies, one guinea, if *you* go to the doctor; two guineas if the doctor goes to *you*.'

He spent much of May and June in bed, and was only able to 'toddle out' with the aid of a stick; his brains were so 'muddled' that he was not able to continue work on his new novel. Yet by the end of July he was well enough to accept an invitation from Dickens to spend a month or two with the Dickens family in Boulogne; Dickens had rented a villa here, on the side of a steep hill overlooking the town, and it seemed to be the ideal spot for recuperation from long illness. Collins was lodged in the upper half of a small pavilion in the grounds, from which he ventured into the town itself where he was once found eating pâté de foie gras for breakfast. He was diverted by French wines as well as by French cookery. In his letters Dickens mentions visits to the local theatre as well as attendance at the various Sunday fêtes and fairs and markets. Yet his guest also found time to work on his uncompleted manuscript, and managed to complete several chapters of *Hide and Seek*.

While in Boulogne Collins sketched out a long European holiday with Dickens and with a fellow guest, Augustus Egg, to be undertaken in the autumn of the same year. Egg was a gentle, quiet and good-natured man who could act as a suitable foil for the sharp and decisive Dickens. This was to be a glorious journey, the nineteenth-century equivalent of the Grand Tour, taking in France, Switzerland and Italy – from Paris to Geneva, from Milan to Naples, from Rome to Venice.

Dickens was invariably the leader whose energy and purposefulness would have irritated less tractable companions. He was the inspirer, the organiser, of the enterprise. 'I lose no opportunity', he informed his sister-in-law, 'of inculcating the lesson that it is of no use to be out of temper in travelling.' Consequently, as Collins wrote to his mother, 'we travel in a state of mad good spirits, and never flag in our jollity all through the day'. The note of overstrained gaiety is quite familiar in any account of Dickens's company. 'We observe the Managerial punctuality in all our arrangements,' he told his wife, 'and have not had any difference whatever.' Dickens of course was the Manager.

So he hurried them along. 'I am so restless to be doing – and always shall be, I think, so long as I have any portion in Time – that if I were to stay more than a week in any one city here, I believe I should be half desperate to begin some new story!'

They started off from Boulogne by railway to Paris, and found the French capital full of English travellers; from Paris they travelled by rail to Strasbourg and then on by carriage into Switzerland, the landscape of which furnished fresh material for Collins's descriptive pen. He did not care for the hotels or the landlords, however; at Basel the hotelier looked like an undertaker, and treated his guests accordingly. In Lausanne the little party visited a school for the deaf and blind; Collins, who at the time was creating a profoundly deaf heroine, was more than usually interested.

From Lausanne they went on to Geneva, and from Geneva to Chamonix 'in a queer little box called a char, drawn by a mare and a mule' which shook and rattled so much on the stony roads that 'my very jaws clatter and my feet play a perpetual tattoo on the bottom of the char'. On the following morning, after their arrival at Chamonix, Dickens led them on an ascent of the Mer de Glace through deep snow. Collins was by now thoroughly discomfited, even if he took care not to show it to his companions. He had, after all, only just recovered from a serious illness. Towards the end of their time in Switzerland he was obliged to take to his bed for two days.

We have the advantage of Dickens's letters to throw light upon Collins. 'He takes things easily,' he told his wife, 'and is not put out by small matters.' Also he 'eats and drinks everything, gets on very well everywhere, and is always in good spirits'. His only fault was that 'he sometimes wants to give people too little for their troubles'. He was, in other words, parsimonious. In homage to their foreign and exotic surroundings Dickens proposed that they should all grow moustaches; it was then considered that shaving was the mark of respectability and Collins enquired, four years later, whether 'the most trustworthy banker's clerk in the whole metropolis have the slightest chance of keeping his situation if he left off shaving his chin'? Dickens's moustache grew luxuriant, but those of Collins and of Egg did not 'take'. Dickens compared that of Collins to the eyebrows of his one-year-old child. It was yet another mark of the older novelist's superiority.

Italy was the true destination of the three men and, as soon as they crossed the Simplon Pass, Collins began palpably to relax. At their first stop over the border, in Domodossola, he was delighted by the food which he considered to be infinitely superior to that of Switzerland. And the wine was only eighteen pence a bottle. He was back in the country he had visited when he was a schoolboy fifteen years before; the flood of powerful memories was such that, when listening to a blind Italian fiddler singing Italian songs, Collins was almost moved to tears. He also heard 'that sort of chaotic and purposeless general screaming which constitutes the staple of ordinary Italian conversation'.

On the journey to Milan in an ancient carriage they were advised to attach a length of string to their luggage which could then be held; this would alert them to any attempt to steal it. So 'we held out three impromptu bell ropes all the way to Milan. It was like being in a shower-bath and waiting to pull the string.' Augustus Egg, a significant and serious painter of the Victorian world, had come in part to see the art; he and Collins would converse about the work they saw, much to Dickens's impatience; he had no particular interest in the Old Masters, and considered artistic discourse be so much humbug. 'To hear Collins learnedly holding forth to Egg (who has as little of that gammon as an artist *can* have) about reds, and greens, and things "coming well" with other things, and lines being wrong, and lines being right, is far beyond the bounds of all caricature.' Dickens was also mildly irritated by Collins's general untidiness; while Dickens lived in perfect neatness and order, Collins's room was always messy with random objects strewn all over the place.

Over the next six weeks they made their Grand Tour of the country, with stops in Genoa, Naples, Rome and Venice. The steamboat from Genoa to Naples was overbooked and the three companions were obliged to spend the first night on the deck along with other passengers who were arrayed, in Dickens's evocative phrase, like 'spoons in a sideboard'. Dickens managed to obtain a cabin on the following night, while Collins and Egg 'pigged together' in a storeroom. In Naples Collins met an acquaintance from the previous trip. Did you not break your arm? No, my brother did. 'Galway's dead.' Galway was the boy responsible for Charles Collins's injury. While in Naples they found time to climb to the crater of Mount Vesuvius where Collins saw 'a blood-red setting sun gleaming through the hot vapour and sulphur smoke'.

Rome was exactly as Collins remembered it. He recognised all his old haunts on the Pincian Hill. He saw the same bishops with purple stockings, the same men with pointed hats and the same women with red petticoats. The beggars, and the urchins, were always there. He observed the pope, looking anxious and miserable. As the pontiff passed all of the people fell on their knees, except for Collins, who took off his hat; the pope bowed gravely to him. This was the Roman world.

In Venice they entered another landscape. They were met by the gondola of the Hotel Danieli at the railway station and were then whisked across the dark waters of the Grand Canal; with the ancient houses on either side, it seemed to Collins that he might have returned to the Middle Ages. They hired a gondola for the duration of their stay, and attended the opera and the ballet; they lived among pictures and palaces, but the weather was so cold that Collins purchased a voluminous Venetian greatcoat complete with hood.

They returned to England, in December 1853, by way of Lyons and Paris. Collins discovered, when their expenses were shared, that he had spent more than he had intended. It was difficult to be frugal in the company of Dickens. It was necessary for him, however, to attend to business once more. His letters to friends and relatives from the Continent were designed to provide material for a series of travel articles in *Bentley's Miscellany*. So at the beginning of 1854 he put together the first instalment of 'Letters from Italy' and delivered it to Bentley's office. Unfortunately a series on the same subject, 'A Journey from Westminster to St Peter's', had only just finished in the *Miscellany*; Collins had not concerned himself to check, and was thus doubly disappointed by the rejection. He may have then offered the series to *Household Words* but, if so, Dickens did not accept it.

In suitably chastened mood Collins then went back to his work on the partly completed novel which had been broken off by illness and foreign travel. He worked quickly on it in the early months of the year, and had completed it by the spring. *Hide and Seek* was published by Richard Bentley in June, and dedicated to Charles Dickens 'as a token of admiration and affection'.

It had an enthusiastic reception, since it was considered to be free of 'the close, stifling, unwholesome odour' that had lingered about its predecessor, *Basil*; the anonymous reviewer of the *Leader* praised it for the 'complicated clearness' of its plot, an appropriate phrase for much of Collins's fiction. Dickens told his sister-in-law that 'I think it far away the cleverest novel I have ever seen written by a new hand.' Its reception was not helped by the outbreak of the Crimean War at the end of March. The travails of the war monopolised national attention; the public was more interested in reading newspapers rather than novels. So *Hide and Seek* languished on the outer edges of public consciousness. The first edition was sold but no other appeared.

The dedication was apt enough since the novel has a decidedly Dickensian flavour. Its heroine is a deaf mute known as Madonna, who has lost her senses of speech and hearing while performing an equestrian act at the circus. One of the central protagonists is Valentine Blythe, an artist of 'slight intellectual calibre' who specialises in no particular style; he is married to a woman who is so severely disabled that she cannot rise from her bed. Madonna and Mrs Blythe might fairly be said to represent the restricted lives of the Victorian female, even if Collins was more concerned to illustrate 'the patience and the cheerfulness with which the heavier bodily afflictions are borne'. Another important character is Mat Marksman, who wears a black skullcap to disguise his scalping at the hands of Native Americans; he is looking for the lost daughter of his dead sister who by curious coincidence . . . The novels of Wilkie Collins are bursting with curious coincidences.

The first part of the narrative is devoted to the hiding of secrets, in the course of which Collins attacks all those forms of Victorian convention that had afflicted him in the past, from Sabbatarianism to office work in a tea-importing business. The second part of the narrative concerns the seeking-out of a truth that can only be known when various forms of evidence become available. Such chapter headings as 'The Finding of the Clue', 'The Brewing of the Storm' and 'More Discoveries' suggest the tone.

Hide and Seek is lively and entertaining, which is as much to say that it lacks the intensity and fatality of *Basil*; but it has more incidental colour, with a high-spirited narrative not immune from facetiousness. It is diverting enough, with that element of extreme suspense that Collins can bring to any story. That was his greatest gift. The novel is an extremely well-manufactured device, with an intricate mechanism at its centre. That is why Collins was a master of plot rather than of character.

After his labours on the novel he spent six weeks of the summer once more in Boulogne with the Dickens family. Dickens had written to him from the Villa du Camp de Droite, saying that he would be briefly in London and inviting him to return to France with him. While in the capital he would be ready for 'a career of amiable dissipation and unbounded licence'; Collins was now clearly his companion of choice. They travelled to Boulogne towards the end of July, where they engaged in more domestic pastimes such as playing rounders and flying kites with the children.

The relative failure in the sales of *Hide and Seek*, and the uncertainty of writing fiction against the background of the continuing war, persuaded Collins to consider 'dramatic experiments' as a way of securing future income. His relationship with Richard Bentley was also more precarious; the firm was in financial difficulties, and Richard Bentley had already asked Collins if he might like to buy back the copyrights of *Antonina* and *Basil*; Collins, himself hard-pressed, declined the offer. So he would try his hand at plays. He wrote a short story for the Christmas number of *Household Words* and, to complete the seasonable festivities, he acted in a pantomime with the Dickens children at Tavistock House. Dickens christened him, in recognition of his Italianate proclivities, Wilkini Collini.

Yet his real attention was now given to a melodrama entitled *The Lighthouse*. He already had a plot to hand, in a short story that he had written for *Household Words* two years before. 'Gabriel's Marriage' concerns the estrangement between a son and father, in the son's belief that his father is a murderer; in a twist natural to a Collins narrative, the alleged victim then appears. Collins simply moves the narrative from Brittany to England, and sets it in the Eddystone Lighthouse a century back. The short story also has premonitions of Collins's most famous novel, *The Woman in White*. 'The White Women! The White Women! . . . You'll see them bright as lightning in the darkness, mighty as the angels in their stature, sweeping like the wind over the sea, in their long white garments . . .' Collins was also working on another play, in five acts, adapted from a 'book'; nothing is known of this work, but it may be that he had decided to wring a play out of *Basil* or *Hide and Seek*.

He travelled to Paris with Dickens in February 1855, but became ill soon after his arrival; they were staying in an apartment in the Hôtel Meurice, overlooking the Tuileries, where Dickens described him to his sister-in-law as 'in a queer state'. He went on to say that 'I go out walking all over Paris while the invalid sits by the fire or is deposited in a café.' Yet they still dined in a different restaurant, and went to the theatre, every night.

The nature of the illness is not known, and in his letters to his mother Collins neglects to mention it. There may have been a reason for his reticence, however. On their return to England, Collins not yet fully recovered, Dickens wrote that 'I hope you will soon begin to see land beyond the Hunterian Ocean.' John Hunter, an English surgeon, had written *A Treatise on the Venereal Disease*; the 'ocean' may be a light-hearted reference to the discharge of urethritis or gonorrhoea. Collins was still confined to the house in the middle of March and, in a letter to Ned Ward, he described the illness as 'a long story which I will not bother you with now'. He could manage at the most a half an hour's walk. He was not completely recovered until the middle of April. It is possible, therefore, that he was afflicted by a venereal infection rather than conventional gout or neuralgia; it is well known that certain infections of the genitals can be followed by arthritic symptoms that may last for several months and can flare up repeatedly over many years. Inflammation of the eyes is also common in such cases, if the finger strays from penis to eye. One of the causes of Collins's ill health, therefore, might be an early bout of urethritis.

He worked on *The Lighthouse* through the spring, and in May showed the manuscript to Dickens. The older novelist became so deeply interested in what he called 'a regular old-style melodrama' that he decided to take on the lead role of Aaron Gurnock, a lighthouse keeper who is filled with remorse for his supposed part in a murder; he suffers from what one member of the audience called 'a horrible sense of blood-guiltiness'. Dickens built a stage for its performance in the children's schoolroom at Tavistock House with space for an audience of approximately twenty-five. Rehearsals began within a fortnight of his first reading; they were held at seven each evening, and Dickens's oldest son recalled how carefully his father arranged all the scenic effects. A sheet of iron was used for the rattle of the thunder, and the rolling of cannon balls for the sound of the sea striking the lighthouse itself. Clarkson Stanfield, well known for his sea views, painted the scenery. There was even an orchestra. It ran for four nights from 16 June 1855, with a cast including Augustus Egg and Collins himself.

It was a triumph; at least it reduced some of the spectators to tears, which was the next best thing. Dickens remarked that it was 'the chief topic of conversation' at a dinner party given by Lord John Russell. Collins had not achieved the commercial success he had once hoped for but, two years later, *The Lighthouse* was staged at the Olympic on Wych Street by the Strand. It thus became Collins's first professional production, and his career in the theatre formally began.

8

The Secret Life

In the absence of a great 'hit', either fictional or dramatic, Collins was relying for his income on the periodical press. He was writing reviews for the *Leader* and short stories for *Household Words*; in the latter capacity he had begun collaborations with Dickens himself.

In the summer of 1855, after his participation in *The Lighthouse*, he joined the Dickens family at Folkestone. Folkestone was considered to be quieter than Broadstairs, previously favoured by the family as a holiday destination. Collins was not particularly impressed by the summer visitors, however, and concluded that the majority of the female contingent were unattractive women in large and ugly hats. Dickens still took his prodigious walks and had discovered a passion for 'climbing inaccessible places'. It is not clear whether Collins himself was as energetic and as nimble as his fellow novelist.

He took with him a manuscript that his mother had written, concerning her early life before her marriage, in the hope that he might be able to batter it into a shape suitable for publication. He did not prove successful but he may have used one of her motifs – a modest painter supported by a resourceful wife – to introduce a series of short stories, all but one taken from *Household Words*. By reprinting the stories in volume form, in a collection of his own work entitled *After Dark*, he earned a double financial consideration.

In the early autumn of the year he allowed himself another holiday in the company of Edward Pigott; Pigott was a keen and able sailor and invited Collins to join him on a yacht he had rented at Bristol. They hired three brothers from the docks there to be their crew, and during the month of September they sailed along the Cornish coast and visited the Scilly Isles. He was an excellent sailor, never once succumbing to seasickness, and this mode of transport became his fashion. The sea was always his 'old old friend'. It was handy, for a lazy man, to be carried from place to place in comfort. He was not troubled by importunate and boring visitors; he was not pestered by the post. Collins suggested that some of the provisions should be purchased at Fortnum & Mason's, thus ensuring the quality of what in other circumstances might be called rations. The preserved meat paste, in particular, was known to be excellent.

Always ready to use material close at hand, he reworked the sailing expedition and turned it into his first non-fiction contribution to *Household Words*; 'The Cruise of the Tomtit' is a celebration of life on board a small yacht. 'We are a happy, dawdling, undisciplined, slovenly lot. We have no principles, no respectability, no stake in the country, no knowledge of Mrs Grundy.' 'Mrs Grundy' was the nickname given at the time to the more pious or prudish sensibilities of the Victorian public. It is clear that Collins enjoyed taking a holiday from nineteenth-century conventions.

It may have been in this period, in fact, that he became acquainted with Caroline Graves. The circumstances of their first meeting are shrouded in doubt. One version comes from the son of John Millais. In his account the two Collins brothers and his father were walking back from Hanover Terrace to the house of Millais's parents in Gower Street when 'they were suddenly arrested by a piercing scream coming from the garden of a villa close at hand'. Suddenly the iron gate to the garden was thrown open 'and from it came the figure of a young and beautiful woman dressed in flowing white robes'; she hesitated in front of the three young men, with a look of supplication and terror, and then fled into the shadows.

'I must see who she is and what is the matter,' Wilkie Collins said before hurrying after her. He did not return and, on the following day, seemed strangely reluctant to talk about the experience. He did tell them, however, that she had told him her history. She was a young lady 'of good birth and position' who had been kept captive by an unnamed man in a villa by Regent's Park, where he had mesmerised her and threatened her. In desperation she had finally managed to escape him. The year is unknown. It might have been as early as 1854.

This sounds like a plot of a Collins novel and it is, indeed, hard to take seriously. Millais's memoir of his father was published when all of the participants in the intriguing scene were dead. It is of course possible that Collins himself made up the story as a way of evading the facts concerning Caroline Graves.

She had not been imprisoned in a villa off Regent's Park, nor had she been mesmerised. She was a widow with a young daughter who kept a 'marine store', or shop of assorted small goods, under her original name of Elizabeth or 'Lizzie' Graves. The shop itself was in Charlton Street, Fitzroy Square, and was indeed on the route that took Millais and the Collins brothers from Hanover Terrace to Gower Street. It is possible, to put it no higher, that she had indeed run out in distress for reasons unknown. Nevertheless she remained in her shop for the next two years.

At a subsequent date she claimed that her late husband, George Robert Graves, was 'of independent means'. In fact he was a shorthand writer, or solicitor's clerk. She described her father as 'a gentleman' by the name of Courtenay. He was in reality John Compton, a carpenter from a village near Cheltenham. She also reduced her age, in official documents, by several years. She was in other words liable to take liberties with the truth and to exaggerate her standing in the world. Nevertheless she retained the affection of Wilkie Collins and, except for one brief interval, remained with him for the rest of his life. They now lie buried within the same grave. She may also have been a model for the spirited and intelligent women of his mature fiction.

He seems to have been staying with her in late January and February 1856; in this period he declined Dickens's increasingly urgent invitations to Paris, where the Dickens family and assorted guests were staying. He must have hinted at the truth because in a letter of 10 February Dickens replied that 'I told them at home that you had a touch of "your old complaint" and had turned back to consult your Doctor'; he said this in order to avoid any 'contretemps with your mother on the hand and my people on the other'. Dickens often referred to Caroline Graves, in later correspondence, as 'the Doctor'.

He had told Collins, on inviting him to Paris, that 'it strikes me that a good deal might be done for *Household Words* on that side of the water'. He had decided that he and Collins should explore the more colourful and sensational life of Paris in a series of articles; he had, for example, already been looking at the possibilities of setting up a guillotine. Collins needed the money, of course, and so set off across the Channel at the end of February. Before he left England, however, he witnessed the publication of his first collection of short stories. It had been taken on by Smith, Elder, in a two-volume edition; George Smith had previously declined to publish *Antonina*, but now took the opportunity of snapping up the rising young author. Richard Bentley, and his son George Bentley, would not publish him again for another eighteen years.

After Dark included what may be considered to be the first English detective story, 'A Stolen Letter', a reworking of Poe's 'The Purloined Letter', and also a Poe-like piece of Gothic nonsense entitled 'The Yellow Mask'. The affinity between Collins and Poe has often been observed; both are interested in the possibilities of Gothic fiction, and both have a taste for the macabre and the sensational. They also both dwell on the problems of false or mistaken identity. They were artists of the improbable, by which they maintain the utmost verisimilitude in order to encompass the wildest impossibilities. Like Poe, also, Collins was one of the most calculating of writers and revised continually; unlike Poe, however, he does not manage to touch upon the most universal or deeply rooted fears. There was even a resemblance in physiognomy; Poe had a very high forehead, with a great development of the temple.

One story published at the end of 1855 was too late for inclusion in *After Dark*; 'The Ostler', later retitled as 'The Dream Woman', is a vividly imagined account of a murderous wife, and thus may be said to represent all of Collins's misgivings about the marital state. It was better to keep a mistress, perhaps, than to marry.

When Collins arrived in Paris he found the Dickens family ensconced in an apartment above a carriage factory on the Champs-Elysées. He was lodged in separate accommodation in the grounds, in a pavilion that 'resembles in size, brightness and insubstantiality a private dwelling house in a Pantomime'.

He became ill in Paris once more with 'rheumatic pains and aguish shivering', and was confined to his little bed. From this vantage, surrounded by pills and potions, he could observe the porter's lodge and the animated life of the great street outside the gates. 'If my pavilion had been built on purpose for me to fall sick in with the least possible amount of personal discomfort, it could not have been better contrived.' He watched the quick step and liveliness of the porter's wife; he noticed a nursemaid 'with a hopeless consumptive languor in her movement'; he observed 'a sober brown omnibus, belonging to a sanitary asylum' and he reflected upon the possible ailments afflicting its passengers. Sickness was much on his mind.

Yet he may have been cheered by the good reviews that *After Dark* had garnered. The critic on the *Atlas* commented that 'very few works of fiction that have been sent to us in a long while are half so good' while the *Leader* declared that 'no man tells a better story'. This indeed was his charm; he was born to be a teller of stories. A more substantial account of his work came from Paris itself. At the end of the previous year the French critic Emile Forgues, editor of the *Revue des Deux Mondes*, had written a long and penetrating review of Collins's writing career. He praised his liberal opinions and his hostility to the hypocrisy, prejudice and venality that seemed native to the English; it was obvious that Collins despised 'cant' and 'false Puritanism'. 'I read that article', Collins wrote at a later date, 'at the time of its appearance with sincere pleasure and sincere gratitude, and I have honestly done my best to profit from it ever since.'

Illness did not prevent him from working, however, and he finished a short novel on the career of a charming charlatan. *A Rogue's Life* was written in a gay and artificially bright style that seemed to appeal to the readers of *Household Words*, where it was eventually published. It is the story of Frank Softly, an artist turned forger and then coiner; the man cannot be serious for more than one moment at a time, and Collins conveys all of his vivacious cheerfulness in a narrative that gallops from one adventure to the next. It was another attack by Collins on Victorian respectability. Dickens himself was sure of its worth and told his partner on the periodical, W. H. Wills, to offer Collins £50 for the rights.

While in a state of enforced rest Collins also began planning the plot of his next novel, to be called *The Dead Secret*. He always worked out the structure of his narratives with great care and circumspection. He plotted everything, down to the most minute detail, and then worked backwards to make sure that all fitted together. There is no effect without a cause. He always decided on the end before he began. Even if he put down nothing on paper, he wrote his novel 'in my head'. He had his material; then he meditated upon it, drawing lines of light between the characters, 'jumping into the skins of others', as he put it, while brooding over motives and intentions. His description of Balzac's methods is also a depiction of his own. 'He was not satisfied with possessing himself of the main idea only; he followed it mentally into its minutest ramifications, devoting to that process just that amount of patient hard labour and self-sacrifice which no inferior writer ever has the common sense or the courage to bestow on his work.'

He outlined the plot to Dickens, who immediately became engaged and excited by it. Dickens could not guess the ending, but prophesied that Collins would make a great deal of money out of the project. The two novelists also discussed another theatrical venture. They had been considering the death of one of Harriet Collins's acquaintances, Sir John Franklin, who had led a lost expedition to the Arctic in 1845. It was last seen in the summer of that year, and speculation about its fate remained intense. In 1854 another explorer spoke to Inuit hunters who told him that the unfortunate men had succumbed to cold and to cannibalism. His report provoked outrage at home. This was the context in which Collins and Dickens discussed the possibility of a great melodrama set in the polar wastes.

Collins slowly recovered his health by the liberal use of vapour baths, or so he believed, and was able to take to the town with his illustrious companion. He met many of the most prominent French writers, and admired the 'improvements' to Paris under the direction of Haussmann. He visited the theatres and the galleries and the restaurants; the relationship between the sexes was much freer and easier here than in London. He also made an unexpected discovery. While inspecting one of the innumerable second-hand bookstalls in the city he came upon *Recueil des causes célèbres* by Maurice Méjan. It was essentially a compendium of sensational crimes, one of which became the inspiration for *The Woman in White*.

He left unexpectedly and hurriedly on 10 April; the porter's wife brought a scribbled note from him to Dickens; he did not even have time to pay the bills of the local chemist. It may be that urgent news sent him back to London. Harriet Collins had already moved out of Hanover Terrace, putting the furniture in storage in preparation for another house in Marylebone; she herself had gone into the country, while Charles had taken lodgings in Percy Street. Wilkie might have seemed to be in limbo. Yet he quickly found lodgings in Howland Street, a narrow street just off the Tottenham Court Road and only a few yards from the marine store managed by Caroline Graves. The probability is, therefore, that he was joining her and her young daughter in what was known as a 'furnished apartment'. It may be that, for the sake of propriety, he rented one immediately adjacent to that of Caroline Graves.

They were dreary rooms in a drab street, in one of the most dismal areas of London, very different from the Champs-Elysées and Paris; in these circumstances he succumbed to illness once again. 'I looked out', he wrote later, 'upon drab-coloured walls and serious faces through a smoke-laden atmosphere; and I must admit that I was waited on (so far as the actual house service was concerned) by people whose gloomy countenances seemed unconscious of a gleam of inner sunshine for days and days together.' This is the true London of what he called 'Smeary Street'. He became interested in the plight of a young maidservant who seemed surprised when Collins spoke to her in a civil manner. For her, 'life means dirty work, small wages, hard words, no holidays, no future. No human being ever was created for this.'

One of the fruits of his short stay in Howland Street was an impassioned and powerful short story, 'The Diary of Anne Rodway', in which he gives a vivid insight into the life of the poor. It is in one sense a detective story, with the first female detective in English literature. Anne Rodway is a poor 'plain needlewoman' whose friend is brought home to their lodging house with a fatal blow to the head; she clutches a torn cravat in her hand and, after her death, Anne Rodway uses this clue to find her murderer.

But the interest of the story lies not so much in the intrigue of the plot as in the depiction of the lives of the outcast and the dispossessed.

'I couldn't follow along with you,' she said, looking at her ragged shawl, 'for I haven't a decent suit of clothes to walk in. I wish I could give vent in crying for her, like you; but I can't; all the crying's been drudged and starved out of me long ago. Don't you think about lighting your fire when you get home. I'll do that, and get you a drop of tea to comfort you.'

These are the words of another poor female lodger just before the funeral. And, as Anne Rodway confides to her diary, 'how much harder it seemed to live than to die'. A little earlier she had remarked that 'if I had leisure to grieve, where should I find the courage to face tomorrow?' Dickens, reading the manuscript in a railway carriage, astonished his fellow passengers by bursting into tears. It is in fact one of Collins's finest achievements, and certainly the most remarkable of his short stories. Here he conveys the violence, the misery and the raging discontent bred upon what he once called 'the cruel London stones', with an unflinching study of the daily miseries of the poor. If he had turned it into a novel, with its spare and elliptical prose, it would have been a masterpiece.

9

On the Staff

In June 1856 Collins once more went sailing with Edward Pigott; they hired a boat from the Royal Yacht Squadron and set off for Cherbourg, where they might stock the cabin cellar with fine wine. Two months later Collins was again in France, on this occasion in the company of Charles Dickens. He had accepted an invitation to stay with the Dickens family at the Villa des Moulineaux, where they intended to work together on the new play that Collins had already proposed. It was to be entitled *The Frozen Deep*, a romance in three acts. Collins wrote the dialogue, which Dickens then revised for his own theatrical purposes. They had been planning to spend at least two months on the work, but a sudden outbreak of cholera in Boulogne obliged the household to sail back hurriedly to England at the end of August. They had progressed far enough, however, to allow Dickens to send instructions about the painting of the sets.

On his return, Collins went to a new house. Harriet Collins had leased a property on Harley Place off Upper Harley Street, close to the New Road (now the Marylebone Road) and not a million miles from their previous dwelling in Hanover Terrace. It is likely that Caroline Graves and her daughter remained, for the time being, in Howland Street.

The joint labours of Dickens and Collins on *The Frozen Deep* marked the beginning of the period of their most intense collaboration. Dickens seems to have been generally startled and moved by 'The Diary of Anne Rodway', in particular, and in the early autumn of the year offered him a place on the staff of *Household*

Words at a salary of five guineas a week. 'He is very suggestive,' he told his editorial partner, W. H. Wills, 'and exceedingly quick to take my notions. Being industrious and reliable besides, I don't think we should be at an additional expense of £20.00 in the year. By this he meant that, as a paid member of staff, Collins would not be reimbursed for his contributions. He was sure that the younger novelist, 'fighting to get on', would be strengthened by the association with his periodical.

Collins himself was not so certain. A regimen of writing anonymous articles and short stories, under the aegis of 'the Inimitable' – especially since every page of the journal had the subheading 'Conducted by Charles Dickens' – might not be as advantageous as Dickens thought. Might not his work be confused with that of the more prominent novelist? Dickens promptly replied to Wills that 'such a confusion of authorship . . . would be a far greater service than disservice to him. This I plainly see.' Still Collins demurred. He agreed to join the periodical only on condition that it serialised his next novel under his own name. It was an admirable arrangement, testifying to Collins's skill in matters of business. Dickens himself was not convinced that a novel by Collins would be a selling proposition, but he instructed Wills to agree to the terms. He did have slight misgivings about his junior partner, however. He once told Wills that Collins sometimes betrayed a tendency to be 'unnecessarily offensive to the middle class'.

So Collins was soon working with Dickens and other stalwarts of *Household Words* on a collaborative story for the Christmas number of the periodical. 'The Wreck of the Golden Mary', the story of a shipwreck, has a concluding chapter written by him. 'I am the captain of the Golden Mary,' Dickens told a friend. 'Mr Collins is the Mate'. Collins was also at the same time engaged on *The Frozen Deep*, another story of mental and physical suffering. He consulted Dickens on every stage of the composition. He travelled down to Gad's Hill Place, Dickens's country house in Kent, only a few days after its purchase.

With Dickens's enthusiastic encouragement the burden of the drama falls on the afflicted figure of Richard Wardour, to be played by Dickens himself with all the passion and energy of his ferocious nature. Wardour is jealous of a rival in love, Frank Aldersley, who happens to be on the same polar expedition; he struggles with his murderous impulses before, in an act of sublime selflessness, sacrificing himself. In the climactic scene Wardour rescues his rival, played by Collins, from the frozen deep. They both grew beards in order to look the part of polar explorers, and Collins became so attached to his that he retained it for the rest of his life.

Dickens lived the role. He took long walks, declaiming his lines. 'Took twenty miles today and got up Richard's words,' he told Collins, 'to the great terror of Finchley, Neasden, Willesden and the adjacent country.' Collins was no doubt less volcanic.

The schoolroom at Tavistock House was once more the centre of operations, with carpenters and plasterers busy among the actors and musicians. All was chaos – or would have been, if it had not been superintended by the master of the house. The dress rehearsal was held on 5 January 1857, followed by four more performances. Dickens was of course incandescent and transcendent. Collins was transfixed. 'This is an awful thing!' he muttered as he was about to be taken up in Dickens's arms for the final scene. And so Dickens speaks out his last words. 'You will remember me kindly for Frank's sake? Poor Frank! Why does he hide his face? Is he crying? Nearer, Clara – I want to look my last at you. My sister, Clara! Kiss me, sister, kiss me before I die!' The audience, and the other actors, wept with Dickens.

A few months later Queen Victoria agreed to attend a private performance of the play at the Gallery of Illustration together with other royals. A newspaper reported that 'Prince Albert wept bitterly, and the Queen and King Leopold sobbed themselves speechless.' Victoria afterwards sent a message through her equerry that 'her Majesty particularly wishes that her high approval should be conveyed to Mr Wilkie Collins'. It was the only note of royal approbation that Collins ever received. Hans Christian Andersen was also at the performance, and was afterwards invited to Gad's Hill Place together with Collins and other guests.

Collins has left a very funny account of the lugubrious writer of fairy stories. The Dane becomes a German, Herr von Müffe, whose conversation was judged to be 'next to impossible, in consequence of his knowing all languages (his own included) equally incorrectly'; but he talked constantly, and 'shed tears several times in the course of the evening'. His shabby clothes were offset by a large collection of foreign orders of merit pinned to his jacket, and he carried his money and jewellery in one of his boots for fear of robbers. He drank gin and sherry mixed in a tumbler. 'He hung about the house and garden in a weak, pottering, aimless manner, always turning up at the wrong moment, and always attaching himself to the wrong person.' He amused himself by cutting out little figures of shepherds and shepherdesses in paper, and then presenting them to the ladies. He also gathered 'countless nosegays' which he gave out to astonished schoolboys and labourers whom he met. The whole essay is a testimony to Collins's propensity for comic narrative.

By the terms of the agreement which Collins had reached with Dickens, his next novel was now to be serialised in *Household Words*. *The Dead Secret*, the ending of which Dickens could not guess, began to appear at the beginning of January 1857 in weekly instalments. It is indeed the story of a secret finally revealed after chapters of suspense and plotting.

Although Collins had worked out the twists and turns of the narrative in great detail, this was the first occasion on which he had written a serial story. Consequently he was obliged to work, as he put it, 'day *and* night' to keep up with the weekly episodes; he was only a fortnight ahead of the printers in the unrelenting race against time. For a while he shut himself up in a retreat in East Sheen, near Richmond Park, so that he might work undisturbed. Yet it was not an entirely uncongenial experience; most of his subsequent fiction would be published in weekly or monthly form.

The instalments in fact allowed him the opportunity to draw out the intrigue, beginning with a very powerful scene beside the bedside of a dying woman; the woman in question was once an actress, and indeed all of the characters in the novel have a strong dramatic flavour. Her maid is prematurely grey. 'What shock had stricken her hair . . . with the hue of an unnatural old age?' A moment later the maid is trembling outside the door of the room of death, asking herself in a whisper, 'Can she have told him?'

It is sufficiently arresting to keep the reader turning the page or waiting in excitement for the next instalment. Every episode ends on a note of expectation. What is the secret of the Myrtle Room? Why does the maid visit an abandoned grave? What are the contents of the hidden letter? Once it is set in motion, the narrative never for a moment stops. This is the true melody of Wilkie Collins. 'Sarah listened, keeping her face still set toward the hall – listened and heard a faint sound behind her. Was it outside the door on which her back was turned? Or was it inside – in the Myrtle Room?' It was all a great success and, when *The Dead Secret* was published in volume form during the summer, sales far exceeded expectations.

Some of the reviewers thought of it as superior hokum, involving 'the power of putting a mass of detached facts into a decisive and appreciable shape'. The *Saturday Review* went on to say that 'the story constantly moves forward and we feel at the end of the chapter that we are one step nearer the end of the search'. What would have seemed familiar to Victorian readers, however, may come as a welcome surprise to a twenty-first-century audience.

Did he now, at the age of thirty-three, consider himself to be middle-aged? That was the word he used to describe a woman 'say a year or two over thirty'. Yet he was already a writer of stature. In this year the literary journalist, Edmund Yates, placed him fourth among contemporary English novelists – just after Dickens, Thackeray and Charlotte Brontë – and stated that 'as a story-teller he has no equal'. 'No barrister or physician ever worked harder at his profession, devoted more time, or thought, or trouble to it, was prouder of it or pursued it with more zeal and earnestness . . .'

In the early autumn of the year Collins and Dickens set off for a 'walking tour' of Cumberland. They had just taken *The Frozen Deep* to Manchester on two succeeding nights, the second performance before 3,000 people who were according to Collins 'electrified'. Collins had also his first taste of theatrical success in the public theatres, when *The Lighthouse* was performed at the Olympic Theatre on Wych Street. He told his mother that there was a 'perfect hurricane' of applause at the final curtain, and that he was obliged to acknowledge the audience from a private box. So there was now opportunity to cool their fevered spirits in the northern air. They also intended to keep a light-hearted journal which would then be published in *Household Words*.

In the first week of September the two men took the train from Euston Square terminus to Carlisle, from where they rode on to the little village of Hesket Newmarket. Dickens had an end in view; he had already decided that he wanted to ascend the great hill known as Carrock Fell a short distance away. Accompanied by the landlord of the inn where they lodged, Dickens and a reluctant Collins set off in heavy rain to begin their climb. The mist descended, and they became lost among the boulders, the scree and the deep heather. Then Collins slipped upon a wet stone and badly strained his ankle, already weakened after a sprain six weeks before. Now drama became reality. Just as Richard Wardour had carried Frank Aldersley in *The Frozen Deep*, so Dickens now took the injured Collins in his arms and carried him to a dog cart.

Despite the fact that Collins could hardly walk the pair moved on to Wigton and to Allonby; Lancaster, Leeds and Doncaster were also part of their route. The innkeeper's book for the Ship Inn, Allonby, still survives with its entry for their expenses. Lunch on 9 September was accompanied by beer, wine and whisky, at a total cost of nine shillings. Collins's ankle was wrapped in a dirty flannel waistcoat, and he had perpetually to anoint it with a lotion of liniment; Dickens carried him in and out of the carriages they hired at every stage. After a few days he was able to move around with the help of two thick sticks. They kept up the journal, working on it after breakfast; Dickens then went on long walks, while Collins rested in the relative comfort of the inns and hotels at which they stayed. A fortnight after they had begun their journey Dickens returned to London, while Collins travelled to Scarborough where he might more easily recuperate.

'The Lazy Tour of Two Idle Apprentices', published in *Household Words* during the autumn of 1857, is interesting principally for the light it throws upon the relationship between the two novelists. Dickens had undertaken the northern journey partly in order to see Ellen Ternan, the young actress with whom he had become violently infatuated. She would be acting in Doncaster during their visit to the town. So part of the dialogue between 'Thomas Idle' (Collins) and 'Francis Goodchild' (Dickens) in the story becomes pertinent. Dickens remarks that it was no trouble to fall in love.

Collins: 'It's trouble enough to fall out of it, once you're in it.

So I keep out of it altogether. It would be better for you if you did the same.'

Immediately they began work on their next joint venture for *Household Words*. 'The Perils of Certain English Prisoners' was the principal attraction of the Christmas edition of 1857; it draws upon Dickens's ferocious reaction to the Indian Mutiny of that year, when the accounts of the massacre of the English reached him, and was supposed to celebrate the heroism of the English as opposed to the vindictive treachery of the Indians. Collins persuaded him that the native revolt should be set on an imaginary island in the Caribbean rather than in India and, in his contribution, he mitigated the racist frenzy of his collaborator with a narrative at once more comic and more sympathetic. As *The Moonstone* would later demonstrate, he did not share the imperialist arrogance of his contemporaries.

In the spring of 1858 he became ill once more and was advised by his doctor to abstain from work and to recuperate in the country. In accordance with this advice he took a sailing trip to Wales in the early summer, where he encountered an old Welsh bard who screeched songs at him in falsetto; in the following month he could be found at Broadstairs. This was his first extended visit to the seaside town, which would become a perennial favourite. It was still a quiet fishing village, built upon steep chalk cliffs that overlooked a semicircular bay with pleasant sands and a short wooden pier. The principal considerations, however, were its quietness and seclusion. His brother, and Edward Pigott, were with him at 3 Prospect Place; it is highly probable that Caroline Graves and her daughter were of the party, although of course there is no mention of them in his letters to his mother. He exulted in the sea air, and even hired a lugger to cross the Channel. By the second week in August he was almost recovered.

His ill health did not prevent him from writing more short stories and articles for *Household Words*, some twenty in total for this year alone. One of the most interesting, 'The Unknown Public', reveals his alert sense of what might be called the literary market. He lived through a period in which the audience for fiction was rapidly widening, and when novels themselves were increasing in importance. Trollope averred that 'we have become a novel-reading people . . . from the Prime Minister down to the last-appointed scullery maid'. Novels had become the repository of the dreams and ideals, the fantasies and the speculations, of the nation. The abolition of taxes on paper, and such advances in printing technology as the hot-metal composing machine, led to a vast increase in the production of books. Four times as many novels were published in 1850 than in 1820. So everything worked together.

The circulating libraries needed the conventional three-volume novel, known as a 'three-decker'. These were the libraries where, for a subscription of a guinea, a single book could be borrowed at a time; a subscription of two guineas would earn the right of borrowing four books at a time. The railway bookstalls, however, wanted cheap reprints in a single volume. These were the 'yellow-backs'. Sometimes they were also known as 'shilling shockers'. The customer wanted something sensational to read on the train. The popular weekly newspapers, such as the *London Journal* and the *Family Herald*, were also beginning to serialise fiction. It was, as Collins himself remarked, 'a great age for authors'. Authorship became a profession, and the Society of Authors was established towards the end of Collins's life. The trade of literary agent was instituted in the 1870s.

He had also noticed, while walking about the poorer neighbourhoods of London, that the windows of the shops of tobacconists and stationers displayed a quantity of small quarto publications. They became the subject of 'The Unknown Public' in *Household Words*. They 'seemed to consist merely of a few unbound pages; each one of them had a picture on the upper half of the front leaf, and a quantity of small print on the under'. When he travelled about England, he noticed the same phenomenon. Who was buying these penny journals? Then it occurred to him that there was indeed an unknown public for low literature, perhaps amounting to many millions of people. These were not the customers of the book clubs or the circulating libraries or the railway bookstalls; these were not the readers of book reviews in the more important periodicals. He repeats a conversation a customer might have with a stationer.

> Stationer: Some likes one, and some likes another. They're all good pennurths. Seen this one?
> Customer: Yes.
> Stationer: Seen that one?
> Customer: No.
> Stationer: Look what a pennurth!

Collins was far from condemning or disparaging this newly discovered public. It was necessary only to teach it how to read. He had an implicit faith in the Victorian law of progress. 'When that public shall discover its need of a great writer, the great writer will have such an audience as has never yet been known.' There can be little doubt that Collins himself aspired to that position. He liked to invoke the notion of 'King Public'. When he was once told that his novels were read 'in every back-kitchen in England' he considered it to be a compliment rather than an insult. He was always attempting to find new ways of appealing to the public; he wrote with its tastes at the very front of his mind and imagination. Even towards the end of his life he was eager to engage the attention of 'the halfpenny public'.

His understanding of theatrical taste, however, was perhaps a little old-fashioned. Buoyed by the success of *The Frozen Deep* and *The Lighthouse*, he now wrote a play designed expressly for the public stage. In the autumn of 1858 *The Red Vial* opened at the Olympic, the venue for *The Lighthouse* in the year before. Frederick Robson took the lead roles in both *The Lighthouse* and *The Red Vial*. The reviews of the earlier production were kind rather than enthusiastic, the critic for *The Times* describing it as 'a dramatic anecdote rather than an actual drama'. *The Red Vial* was of the same melodramatic temper, concerning a lady poisoner and a German halfwit who is rescued from an insane asylum.

Almost as soon as the curtain rose the audience began to laugh, even though the play was described by Henry Morley as 'two hours of unbroken solemnity'. When the arm of a 'corpse' starts to wave about, and is seen searching for the handle of an alarm bell, the audience erupted in hysterics. Morley, one of the first professors of English Literature, considered Collins's characters to be 'mere puppets, uttering commonplace sentiments tediously expressed'. The play was withdrawn after a few performances and never seen again. In a manuscript of the dialogue Collins wrote that 'Poor little Robson did his best. The rest is silence.' The supper party afterwards at the house of Dickens was described by one guest as a case of funeral baked meats.

In the course of 'The Unknown Public' Collins had also thrown an interesting light on Victorian civilisation with a disquisition on the advice columns of the cheap press. 'Married women who have committed little frailties, consult the editor. Male jilts in deadly fear of actions for breach of promise, consult the editor.' You should not shake hands with a lady on your first introduction to her. You can sell ointment without a patent. A reader wants a recipe for gingerbread while others want cures for grey hair, warts, nervousness and intestinal worms. Another reader wished to know what an esquire is, and another wished to know how to pronounce 'picturesque' and 'acquiescence'. Yet another wishes to know the right hour of the day at which to visit a newly married couple. Is there any inconsistency in being a dancing mistress as well as a teacher at a Sunday School? Can I sell lemonade without a licence? I have been in love with a woman for four years, and have not yet mentioned it to her. Please advise.

10

The Woman

At the end of 1858 Collins moved with his brother and mother to a new house in the neighbourhood of Regent's Park, 2 Clarence Terrace. Yet a more important address was now also his. By the beginning of 1859 he is writing letters with '124 Albany Street' at their head. Caroline Graves had been registered as a ratepayer in this residence, also close to Regent's Park, in 1858; she was noted as 'Mrs Graves'.

He was now clearly living with Caroline Graves while also residing, for the sake of appearances, at Clarence Terrace. He must also have been paying the rent and the rates. In Albany Terrace they received such guests as Edward Pigott and Augustus Egg, but they would have been shunned by the more respectable of their acquaintance. No married lady would have visited them. There will have been friends who deplored this connection, and urged him to break it. There may have been others who considered Caroline Graves to be an adventuress or worse. If Caroline Graves and Collins gave dinner parties, no ladies would be invited. Parents would have forbidden children to play with Caroline Graves's daughter, Harriet, known as 'Carrie'.

Collins himself alludes to the difficulties of an unmarried couple in many passages. In one novel, *Armadale*, he reflects that 'the influence exercised by the voice of public scandal is a force which acts in opposition to the ordinary law of mechanics. It is strongest, not by concentration, but by distribution.' In *The New Magdalen* a character writes that 'people who in former years habitually called upon me and invited me – or who, in the event of my absence, wrote to me at this season – have abstained with a remarkable unanimity from calling, inviting, or writing now'. Another character, in *No Name*, sums up the situation. 'I have lived long enough in this world to know that the Sense of Propriety, in nine English women out of ten, makes no allowances and feels no pity.'

There will also have been problems with servants and landlords. It may have been some altercation, for example, that prompted the removal of Collins and Caroline Graves to another house in the immediate neighbourhood. At 2a New Cavendish Street they took rooms from a local doctor, who may have been more sympathetic than most about their circumstances.

In the summer of 1859 they went once more to Broadstairs where for six weeks they rented a house, Church Hill Cottage, on the Ramsgate Road. It was a quiet location, with a clear view of the sea from the downs; he liked to watch the various vessels as they passed perpetually. He hired a cook, but had to deal with assorted tradesmen who drove hard bargains with the visitors. Collins discovered to his horror that vegetables were three times the price of those sold in London. Certain guests, Charles Ward and Charles Collins among them, came to stay; Dickens took rooms at a nearby inn.

Yet for much of the time Collins was at his desk, working from ten until two each day. Even now he had begun the composition of his new serial novel. He told Ward that 'the story is the longest and most complicated I have ever tried yet – and the difficulties at the beginning of it are all but insuperable'. Mental labour was, as always with Collins, accompanied by physical ailments; he was suffering from a painful boil between his legs that the local doctor was obliged to lance. 'I seem destined, God help me! never to be well.'

He had composed a mass of notes for the new novel and had outlined the plot in great detail before a word of it had reached the printer. The central idea, as he put it, was 'a conspiracy in private life, in which circumstances are so handled as to rob a woman of her identity by confounding her with another woman sufficiently like her in personal appearance to answer the wicked purpose'. He derived the idea from one of the books he had picked up in Paris, Méjan's *Recueil des causes célèbres*. This was an account of a French widow who found herself in a mental institution in Paris, under an assumed name, after being drugged by her brother. The estate of the widow, presumed dead after an interval, was bestowed upon the wicked sibling. So true events are given an imaginative purpose.

Collins originally set the beginning of the narrative in Cumberland, but then changed his mind. He read in the newspaper of a patient escaping from a mental asylum. The vista of Hampstead, and the Heath, came before him. 'There in the middle of the broad, bright high-road – there, as if it had that moment sprung out of the earth or dropped from the heaven – stood the figure of a solitary Woman, dressed from head to foot in white garments; her face bent in grave enquiry on mine, her hand pointing to the dark cloud over London, as I faced her.'

He still needed a title. The North Foreland lighthouse, just a short walk away, seems to have provided the inspiration. It glowed white in the evening light, its beams flashing out to sea. 'You are ugly and stiff and awkward; as stiff and as weird as my white woman. White woman! Woman in White!' He may also have remembered the 'white women' who were invoked in his short story 'Gabriel's Marriage'; that story in turn became *The Lighthouse*. So associations and connections are formed without conscious intention. In the same period a select committee of Parliament had been established for an 'inquiry into the care and treatment of lunatics and their property'. Public events, and private purposes, came together. Collins was always fascinated by madness, and in 1861 was given Forbes Winslow's *On Obscure Diseases of the Brain and Disorders of the Mind* with an inscription from the author; it is probable that he consulted Winslow on certain matters.

Just before *The Woman in White* began its publication in *All the Year Round*, a second collection of his short stories appeared in print. *The Queen of Hearts* contains some of Collins's finest stories, principal among them 'The Diary of Anne Rodway'. In this branch of his art he was unsurpassed. As one of the characters in the book puts it, 'what I want is something that seizes hold of my interest, and makes me forget when it is time to dress for dinner – something that keeps me reading, reading, reading, in a breathless state to find out the end'. That is precisely the excitement that Collins conveys to his readers. On some occasions he may have succeeded all too easily. One reviewer of this volume described him as 'a machinist'; if he was, he was a machinist of genius.

The Woman in White began its serial career at the close of November 1859 in the number of *All the Year Round* in which *A Tale of Two Cities* was concluded. Two great novels of sensation thereby came together. *All the Year Round* was Dickens's new periodical venture, he having had an acrimonious dispute with his previous publisher. So he needed work that would command a wide readership. With Collins he had found the best possible contributor.

The arresting opening of *The Woman in White*, and the intriguing mystery of its plot, ensured that the serial had a wide and immediate appeal. Queues of eager readers would line up outside the offices of the periodical on Thursday mornings to purchase the newly printed episode. It can be said with some certainty that Collins's novel helped to guarantee the enormous increase in sales. *Household Words* had managed sales of between 36,000 and 40,000 copies; *All the Year Round* never dipped below 100,000.

The Woman in White seized the public imagination as its

William Collins,
engraving from the
portrait by John Linnell.

Harriet Collins, by John Linnell.

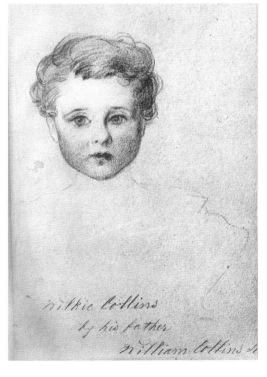

Wilkie Collins aged one,
probably drawn by his father.

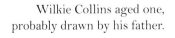

Wilkie in 1857,
by Herbert Watkins.

Charles Collins, 1850.

Charles Dickens, 1852.

Charles Fechter.

The Gallery of Illustration cast of *The Frozen Deep*, July 1857.
Wilkie Collins is leaning forward behind the front row,
towards the right, with Dickens lying in the foreground.

John Millais,
Frontispiece to *No Name*, 1864.

Arthur Hopkins' illustration to *The Haunted Hotel*, 1889.

Caroline Graves in the 1870s.

Wilkie with
Martha Rudd.

Ramsgate harbour.

Nannie Wynne in the 1880s.

Wilkie in the 1880s, by Alexander Bassano.

arresting and on occasions breathtaking narrative unfolded. What is the mysterious past of Anne Catherick? Why does she always dress in white? What is her connection with the half-sisters, Marian Halcombe and Laura Fairlie? Why had she been kept in an asylum and why is she so terrified of Sir Percival Glyde? We know that these questions will in due time be answered, and yet we burn with curiosity and anticipation. And all the while Collins contrived hundreds of what he called 'connecting links' which maintain the smoothness and reality of the whole illusion; on each successive perusal, the reader discovers further subtleties and connections.

As he worked on it week by week he once again suffered intermittently from ill health; earache was tormenting him. Yet still he pressed on, engaged in what he called his weekly race with the press. There were one or two diversions. In the spring he moved with Caroline around the corner to 12 Harley Street. While in the throes of composition he had to deal with plumbers, carpenters and the assorted difficulties of moving house. He hired two servants, and arranged for a fresh supply of headed notepaper. Caroline was now known to the world as 'Mrs Collins'. In the census return Harriet or 'Carrie' Graves becomes Harriet Montague, a house servant. This subterfuge may have been designed to placate their landlord, a dentist, who also lived on the premises.

Dickens had visited what he described as 'the handsome and comfortable' rooms in Harley Street, but referred somewhat disparagingly to 'the (female) skeleton in that house'. He had taken a dislike to her, and never spoke of her to his friend. He hoped only that Collins had no intention of marrying her.

In the middle of July 1860 Charles Collins married Dickens's daughter, Kate, at Gad's Hill where Collins and his mother were among the guests. It was not a very cheerful affair. Dickens believed that his daughter was getting married only to escape from him, and he regarded his son-in-law with suspicion as a weak-willed and dilatory individual; he may also have believed him to be impotent or even homosexual. There were no speeches and, at the end of the day, Dickens was found sobbing into his daughter's wedding dress.

Collins wrote the last episode of the novel just nine days after the wedding, and two weeks later gave an all-male dinner of celebration in Harley Street. 'No evening dress,' he wrote, 'everything in the rough.' Augustus Egg and Holman-Hunt were among the guests. Dickens did not attend; he had told one old friend that Collins had finished *The Woman in White*, and 'if he had done with his flesh-coloured one, I should mention that too'. The reference to Caroline Graves is not exactly flattering.

Collins had originally received an offer from the firm of Sampson Low for the publication rights but then, according to the customary proprieties, he sent it to George Smith for a rival bid. Smith had previously published *After Dark*. Smith had not been following the serialisation of *The Woman in White*, and for some reason was not aware of the furore surrounding it. So he offered £500. At dinner that night a lady beside him asked if he had been 'reading that wonderful novel'. She told him that 'everyone is raving about it. We talk "Woman in White" from morning till night!' He rushed into his office early on the following morning, only to learn that his letter to Collins had already been sent out. The novel went to Sampson Low. Smith confessed later that if he had paid ten times as much as he originally offered, he would have done very well.

The first edition sold out on publication day, and a further five editions were published in the subsequent two months. Thackeray stayed up all night to finish it, and Gladstone cancelled a theatre engagement in order to continue reading it. It was the sensation of the moment. 'Woman in White' bonnets and cloaks were now being sold, as well as 'Woman in White' perfumes; there were 'Woman in White' quadrilles and waltzes. Stories of women in black, in grey, green, blue and every other colour were issued.

The reviews did not seem to reflect the popular success. *The Times* discovered a major flaw in the construction of the plot, the kind of mistake Collins looked upon with horror, while another critic described the author as 'a very ingenious constructor; but ingenious construction is not high art just as cabinet making and joining is not high art'. The reviewer in *The Times* at least had the merit of humour. In the original preface Collins had asked the reviewers not to reveal the end. Not to let the cat out of the bag. *The Times* was incredulous. 'The cat out of the bag! There are in this novel about a hundred cats contained in a hundred bags, all screaming and mewing to be let out. Every new chapter contains a new cat.' Collins contrasted these responses with the enthusiasm of the general public, and decided that the public was right. He may be excused on this occasion for confusing popularity with merit.

It was in fact Collins's most elaborate and ingenious novel to date, in which a succession of mysteries are slowly resolved. In the conspiracies thereby uncovered, the protagonists are equally matched. One of them is 'the exact opposite' of another. It is as if a number of characters were playing chess with each other in some grand tournament of intrigue. Count Fosco is an admirable villain, and Marian Halcombe is a superb heroine. She represents one of the typical Collins characters, as a spirited and clever woman of independent mind. She is also of uncommon appearance. 'The lady's complexion was almost swarthy and the dark down on her upper lip was almost a moustache.'

The Woman in White presents two complex types, the strong-minded and 'masculine' woman as opposed to the ineffectual and 'feminine' man. Some of the male characters are prone to affliction of 'the nerves', for example, and Count Fosco is described as 'nervously sensitive' and 'a fat St Cecilia masquerading in male attire'. The males are often melancholy and passive, while the women are bursting with independence and energy; only the latter are capable of unflinching moral ardour, indeed of ardour at all. The best villains, in his subsequent fiction, are generally women. It is Collins's way of assaulting the sexual conventions and pre-occupations of his time. There are always elements of sexual confusion in his novels. 'Physiology says, and says truly,' a character in *The Moonstone* remarks, 'that some men are born with female constitutions – and I am one of them!'

Men often tyrannise and victimise the women in Collins's fiction, for example, but on almost all occasions the women fight back. That is why, in this story of stolen identity and false imprisonment, Collins is able to dramatise the plight of Victorian women in memorable form; they had no property rights and were deprived of their identity, as wives, while at the same time they were incarcerated in a domestic world. *The Woman in White* thereby became the subject of unsurpassed interest and even fascination.

The technique of the narrative resembles that of a criminal trial in which the various witnesses tell only as much as they know and have no inkling of the general purport of their evidence. Collins said that he had been inspired by his attendance at a real trial, but the merits of the method are clear enough. It encourages suspense and speculation that can only be satisfactorily resolved by the master storyteller himself. It is also a way of emphasising the elusive nature of truth. What is the appearance and what is the reality? What is hidden beneath the surface? A brooding air of gloom, a sense of impending calamity, suffuses the narrative. 'How little I knew then of the windings of the labyrinth which were still to mislead me!' It is a novel of coincidence and double identity, of fatality and suspense. It is a novel of events rather than persons, of plot rather than character. One of Collins's narrators refers to 'the long oppression of the past' and 'the chain' of events. The chain binds all of them together; it imprisons them. 'I felt the ominous Future coming close; chilling me, with an unutterable awe; forcing on me the conviction of an unseen Design in the

long series of complications which had now fastened around us.'
It is a special kind of novel that requires a particular art and a
singular imagination.

It was the first novel by Collins that became known as a 'sensation novel', and he was once described as 'the novelist who invented
sensation'. This may be interpreted in a literal sense. The design
of the sensation novel was 'to electrify the nerves'. The experience
of perpetual suspense may be deleterious to the nervous system;
many of the characters in the novel seem themselves to be in an
hysterical state and may communicate that fever to the reader.
The fact that *The Woman in White* was also first published as a
series intensified its ability to shock and to excite the reader who
waited for the next instalment in a state of breathless anticipation.
But these alarms and tensions may also have disclosed larger fears.
Colllins was writing about mysteries 'deep under the surface' three
decades before Freud began his own enquiries. He was concerned
with doubles and double identity, with monomania and delusion.
He traced the paths of unconscious associations and occluded
memories.

The apparent increase in cases of insanity or 'brain disorder' in
the middle of the nineteenth century was widely noted. One
doctor linked it to the effect of 'a spurious and hollow civilisation'
while the *Edinburgh Review* speculated that it was the result of
intense anxiety and competition in both social and commercial
life; the commentator noted that madness derived from 'the
extreme tension to which all classes . . . are subjected in the
unceasing struggle for position and even life'. The sensation novel
thus complemented a world of rapid and alarming change. Collins's
attacks upon Victorian orthodoxies were part of his awareness of
a greater malaise.

A review in the *Quarterly Review* described the sensation novel
of the 1860s as 'the morbid phenomenon of literature – indica-
tions of a wide-spread corruption . . . called into existence to

supply the cravings of a diseased appetite'. That appetite was provoked by the morbid and the brutal. The novels took their plots from the police courts and the new divorce courts; they were concerned with family secrets, with seductions and bigamies and murders. Collins himself was fascinated by suicide and death by poison. The novels of sensation found vice and melodrama in the suburbs and in the respectable city streets. They exploited the darker aspects of the Victorian world, and were therefore dismissed by moralists as degenerate publications. They were devoted, according to *Punch*, to 'Harrowing the Mind, making the Flesh Creep, causing the Hair to stand on End, Giving Shocks to the Nervous System; destroying the Conventional Moralities; and generally unfitting the Public for the Prosaic Avocations of life'. This is a perfectly reasonable account of *The Woman in White*.

It has remained, for more than 150 years, Collins's most popular novel; and, in the end, he himself knew that it was also his greatest. On his grave at Kensal Green he is identified as 'Author of The Woman in White and other works of fiction'.

11

Hot Brandy and Water

On the conclusion of *The Woman in White* he made plans to escape from his desk. He first went down to Gad's Hill Place to stay with Dickens, and then travelled up by train to Yorkshire in order to visit some friends there. In the early autumn of 1860 he was sailing with Edward Pigott in the Bristol Channel where it rained for two days and blew hard for the rest. He loved the great waves, however, and declared the voyage to be a decided success.

Then in October he travelled to Paris with Caroline, insisting on 'first class all the way, with my own sitting-room in the best hotel when I get there – and every other luxury that the Capital of the civilised world can afford'. He had the means to be more lavish; the success of his latest novel had assured his prosperity. From this time forward he always travelled first class. He was at last earning a respectable income, and in the summer of the year he had opened up his own bank account at Coutts; he had previously used his mother's account for his income and his expenses. Certainly he felt secure enough to finance the education of Carrie Graves at a private academy; she was first of all sent to a boarding school in Surrey. He had also renewed his agreement with *All the Year Round* for two years, thus further securing the immediate future.

He and Caroline were staying at the Hôtel Meurice, from where they ventured out to the restaurants and theatres of the capital. It is likely to have been her first journey abroad, but of course her reactions are not recorded.

On his return he discovered, to his dismay, that an unauthorised dramatisation of *The Woman in White* was about to appear at the Surrey Theatre on the Blackfriars Road in Lambeth. The pirated version lasted only for a short time, however, before the manager withdrew it. Collins would often be plagued by problems of dramatic copyright, since any novel could be dramatised without the consent of the novelist; only if the author arranged for a dramatisation, or organised a semi-public performance, could the rights be preserved. It testifies, if nothing else, to the immense popularity of novels dramatised for the stage.

In the following year Dickens and Collins found that one of their joint collaborations, 'A Message from the Sea', was about to be staged at the Britannia Saloon in Hoxton. On the first night the authors visited the theatre and remonstrated with the manager; he seemed to have accepted the justice of their case, and taken off the play, but then resumed performances. Dickens and Collins had no rights in the matter.

In the winter of 1860 the two novelists had journeyed to Devon in order to collect some local colour for their collaboration on 'A Message from the Sea'. They stayed at a hotel in Bideford where they dined on bad fish. 'No adventures whatever,' Dickens wrote. 'Nothing has happened to Wilkie.' They chose the pretty, if steep, seaside village of Clovelly as the setting for their adventure. Collins was uncharacteristically blocked and spent much of the time staring out of the window. The story he eventually produced, concerning a message in a bottle that causes consternation in a Devonshire fishing village, is not memorable.

At the age of thirty-six Collins had now become something of a literary and social 'lion' with an open invitation to the more artistic circles of London. He sometimes attended, on Saturday afternoons, the musical parties given by George Eliot and G. H. Lewes. He delighted in Mozart, but seems to have disliked Beethoven whose Kreutzer Sonata he described as 'the musical expression of a varying and violent stomach-ache, with intervals of hiccups'. He detested Schumann.

He also became closely acquainted with Nina and Frederik Lehmann, an artistic and gregarious couple who invited Collins to their house in Westbourne Terrace; they were both excellent musicians, the husband on the violin and the wife on the piano. Lehmann had attended the celebratory dinner on the completion of *The Woman in White*, but Collins was equally at home in the company of Nina Lehmann whom he called the 'Padrona'.

He was now prominent enough to play the role of public speaker. In the spring of 1861 he presided at a dinner of the Newsvendors Benevolent Institution, a last-minute substitute for Dickens himself. He turned out to be an engaging and fluent public speaker, and was inclined to exploit 'this newly discovered knack of mine'. Here is the seed of his later public readings of his novels.

His vocation was never for a moment forgotten, even in the round of his daily engagements. By the spring he was engaged in the preparation for his next novel or, as he put it, 'building up the scaffolding of the new book'. He knew that it would be difficult to repeat the success of *The Woman in White*, but he hoped that he might capture the attention of the public with a completely different kind of story.

As he was engaged in these essential preliminaries he received an unexpected and welcome proposal. George Smith, of Smith Elder, having miscalculated the advance for *The Woman in White*, was now determined to recapture the prominent young novelist. He was too late to bid for the next novel which had already been purchased by Sampson Low, but now he offered £5,000 for the fiction that would follow. It was to be published in the *Cornhill*, of which George Smith was the founder, rather than in *All the Year Round* before emerging in volume form. This was larger than any sum Collins had previously received, and he was naturally elated. Only Charles Dickens could command such sums. His future was now fully secure, and he believed himself to be truly 'at the top of the tree' even before reaching the age of forty. Dickens himself was sanguine about Collins's removal to a rival magazine; it was, after all, the considered decision of a fellow professional.

Yet now, ominously, his health took a turn for the worse. His liver was tormenting him. He tried pills, and a change in diet, but then decided to recuperate in a change of air. He visited the Suffolk coast and then, in the early summer, Caroline Graves and he returned to Broadstairs where they stayed at the Albion Hotel with its views across the harbour and Viking Bay; Carrie, out of school, was also with them. He encountered here the familiar seaside scene; middle-aged women were still wearing absurdly youthful straw hats, and the men were still looking through telescopes at nothing in particular. The children still dug in the sand, and the young women read cheap novels, while all around them was the sound of the sea and of the seagulls mewing.

With vistas of the coming book opening in front of him, he next decided to travel north to Whitby where they took rooms at the Royal Hotel. The railway journey across the moors inspired in Collins 'astonishment and admiration'. The hotel itself was high on the west cliff and commanded views of the beaches and the old harbour; their sitting room had three bow windows from which they could survey the boatmen and fishermen below. On the side of the room two more windows opened upon the prospect of the town and the ruined abbey. The place had a grandeur and a wildness that Broadstairs conspicuously lacked.

Yet they discovered that Whitby had its disadvantages. The hotel, if comfortable, was also noisy. One family had fourteen children, and the cacophony was a further irritant to Collins's already strained nerves. A brass band played regularly for four hours each day. He decided that he would never try to work in a hotel again. So the Collins party moved on, while all the time he was looking out for locations in which to set his new novel. They travelled to York and then to Huntingdon, Cambridge and Ipswich before alighting on Aldeburgh.

He noticed here how the sea had encroached upon the land, swallowing up what had once been the streets and marketplace of the old town. The port itself had fallen victim to the waves, and the natives of the place had been forced back upon a strip of land between the marshes and the sea. They had created here what in the novel he would call 'a quaint little watering place', with a line of villas overlooking the dyke which separates them from the sea. Behind them is the one street belonging to the town, 'with its sturdy pilots' cottages, its mouldering marine store-houses and its composite shops'. This was Aldeburgh in the middle of the nineteenth century.

By September they had returned to Harley Street where he could properly work upon his manuscript. Although it was destined for *All the Year Round* Collins had decided that he was now earning more than enough money to leave the staff of the periodical. Dickens took his decision with good grace, realising that his erstwhile protégé was now sturdy enough to support himself. They did not collaborate again for another six years.

By the spring of 1862 the new novel began its public career in *All the Year Round*. The title came, once more, at the last minute. Dickens had made several suggestions but none of them was entirely suitable; at last *No Name* occurred to Collins. He had already shown the early instalments to Dickens who was enthusiastic about the general tone and momentum of the narrative that he had read with interest and admiration. He found one scene, and one character, 'too business-like and clerkly'. This was similar to the one objection he had raised against *The Woman in White*; he believed that the narrators had had a 'DISSECTIVE property in common, which is essentially not theirs but yours'.

Since this was one of the principles of Collins's art, it was not advice that he was disposed to accept.

The novel begins in a light enough key, with a portrait of the Vanstone family at home; mother, father and two daughters are the epitome of respectability. But the mood soon darkens with the death of the father in a train crash; this was one of the horrors of the new age. The report of her husband's death kills Mrs Vanstone, following the premature birth of a son who also dies. The plot now begins to quicken. It transpires that the Vanstones were never married, and that the two sisters are subsequently illegitimate. They have 'no name'. They can inherit nothing. They have no claim. The estate will go to Mr Vanstone's estranged brother.

The reaction of the sisters is very different. Norah Vanstone decides that she will become a governess. Magdalen Vanstone, who has already displayed dramatic propensities, travels to York where she wishes to become an actress. Yet she also decides on revenge. She wishes to reclaim her inheritance by means foul or fair. She will marry the young man, the son of the estranged brother, upon whom her parents' estate has been bestowed. So the scene is set for a drama in which double identity, disguise and suicide all play a part.

Collins had decided to rent Fort House, in Broadstairs, for the summer and autumn so that he might work undisturbed. This was the house on a headland in which Dickens had also stayed for two summers in 1850 and 1851; Collins may have visited the Dickens family in the latter year, and liked what he saw. No doubt he used the same room for a study as his predecessor; it had large windows overlooking the bright sea. The house was too large for him and Caroline Graves but he was, after all, now a substantial man of letters. Ten packages of indispensable items were sent down on the goods train, among them a refrigerator or ice-box. Old friends such as Charles Ward and Augustus Egg took up some of the bedrooms, and he went sailing once more with Edward Pigott. Yet all was not as well as it seemed. He quarrelled with his two servants; both left his service, either because they were dismissed or because they gave in their notice.

It is perhaps significant that his doctor, Frank Beard, was one of his guests. By September Collins's big toe had turned scarlet and had swollen to the size of a small fist. He felt very ill. 'Don't seem to notice it,' Dickens told his sub-editor, W. H. Wills, 'for he is nervous.' He was now working under pressure; his publishers wanted him to complete the narrative by October or November, in time for publication in December, but he did not think he would be able to finish it until the end of the year or even the end of January. He sent out a series of letters, to friends in London, seeking out information for the twists and turns of the narrative. How long did letters take from London to Zurich in 1847? How long was the sea voyage from London to Hong Kong? Tell me about the landscape of Dumfries. Flat or hilly? It is not that he distrusted his imagination. But he knew that readers would persist in sending him letters and putting him right. Accuracy in detail also helped to authenticate his sometimes improbable plots.

At the beginning of October Collins wrote to Beard asking him to come down to Broadstairs. He was afflicted by a general faintness, accompanied by sickness and trembling. He could not sleep and the slightest noise startled him. It may be that his severe hard work had helped to exacerbate these symptoms. He came back to London as soon as he could, in the fear that a sudden breakdown in his health would seriously impair his work on the book. He was confined to his bed for a while and his general ill health was followed by rheumatism and a bad liver. Beard recommended quinine and potassium as well as the ever potent mixture of opium and alcohol known as laudanum. Collins was in any case living in an unhealthy city of fogs and rain and damp; it was a dank and dirty city, of coughs and colds, in which no one was ever wholly well.

Dickens heard the news of Collins's ill health from Frank Beard, who was also his own doctor, and promised to assist Collins; he also had known the fear of not being able to complete successive instalments in time and he assured Collins that, if necessary, he would do the work himself. 'I could do it, at a pinch, so like you as that no-one should find out the difference.' The offer was well meant but perhaps a little insulting; it suggested that there was nothing unique to Collins's style that could not immediately be copied and manufactured.

At the beginning of November Collins told his mother, who was now living permanently out of London in Tunbridge Wells, that he had 'cold in the head, cold in the throat, cold in the chest'. The only remedy seems to have been hot brandy and water. Yet his professionalism was such that he struggled on and never missed any deadline. He even wrote in bed, sometimes dictating the lines to Beard himself. He was still very weak in the middle of the month, but at last finished *No Name* on Christmas Eve at two o'clock in the morning. He had pulled through.

The nervous terrors and general faintness may have been in part due to the laudanum that Beard prescribed. The drug took away, or helped to alleviate, the intense pain of what he believed to be rheumatism and gout. It was widely available as a patent medicine in such concoctions as 'Battley's Drops' and 'Mother Bailey's Quieting Syrup', and could be bought at threepence an ounce in many shops. Like gin in the eighteenth century it helped to alleviate the misery of life. It encouraged dependency, however, and few were able to wean themselves from helpless resort to the drug. Collins was prescribed laudanum by Beard in 1861 or 1862, and was never subsequently free of it. He did in fact take larger and larger quantities, until it was said that he could swallow in a single glass enough to kill twelve people.

He might have been said to have joined the company of De Quincey and Coleridge, except that he was entirely free of their extravagance and self-pity. He never considered himself to be one of a doomed race; he was simply an invalid in need of relief. In fact he was inclined to praise laudanum. One of his characters asks: 'Who was the man who invented laudanum? I thank him from the bottom of my heart, whoever he was. If all the miserable wretches in pain of body or mind, whose comforter he has been, could meet together to sing his praises, what a chorus it would be!' The sentiment is that of Collins himself. He also believed that the drug had a stimulating, as well as a sedative, effect. It cleared the brain and composed the mind.

Yet in the end it had a degenerative effect and became a serious addictive rather than a restorative. On a journey to Switzerland he discovered that the chemists of the country could only supply a limited measure of the drug; his travelling companion had to visit four separate establishments to make up the amount that Collins needed. In later life, too, he began to suffer from nervous hallucinations as a result of his addiction. A second Wilkie Collins sat at the desk with him, trying to take control over the writing pad, struggling with him until the inkstand was upset. Then the 'real' Collins woke up. When he ascended the stairs at night he was confronted by a swarm of ghosts who tried to push him down. Sometimes he saw a woman with green tusks, and sometimes a monster with 'eyes of fire and big green fangs'.

One of the characters in *The Moonstone*, Ezra Jennings, laments that 'even the virtues of opium have their limit. The progress of the disease has gradually forced me from the use of opium to the abuse of it; I am feeling the penalty at last. My nervous system is shattered; my nights are nights of horror.' This may not have been the precise condition of Collins's nerves but it must represent what he most feared; his fragility, and susceptibility, would then have terrified him. It was a moral, as well as a physical, failing.

His will and his judgement would have been affected. It was weak and humiliating.

The first edition of *No Name* consisted of 4,000 copies; by the evening of publication day, only 400 were left. 'Literary gossip', the *Morning Advertiser* reported, 'assigns an almost fabulous sum to the clever writer for this able work.' Its success even merited a parody, *No Title* by Bret Harte. The response of the reviewers was not quite so enthusiastic. the *Reader* said that 'with us, novels turn upon the vicissitudes of legitimate love and decorous affection; while in France they are based upon the workings of those loves and passions which are not in accordance with our rules of respectability'. Collins was of the unpleasant French school.

Collins had introduced the subject of illegitimacy, after all, and his female protagonist is adept at impersonation and deceit. How could she be a Victorian heroine? Yet she is undoubtedly a Collins heroine. She is, in his words, 'resolute and impetuous, clever and domineering; she is not one of those model women who want a man to look up to and protect them – her beau ideal (though she may not think it herself) is a man she can henpeck'. This is a woman who is resourceful and determined, quite unlike the Victorian stereotype of 'the angel in the house'.

All the resources of Collins's art go into the portrayal of Magdalen Vanstone who is at once ferocious, vindictive and high-spirited; she is also remorseful even as she plans her greatest coup of marriage to the enemy, and at one stage contemplates suicide as she looks out to sea at Aldeburgh. If an even number of ships passes by, she will live; if not, she will die. It is one of the most remarkable scenes in what is by any standards an intriguing and eventful novel.

His portrayal of Magdalen, and of other women, has led certain critics to suggest that he was a feminist before his time. The story of a young woman who must battle and defeat the whole world of Victorian propriety must have appealed to those women (and men) who were weary of the conventions. The fact that she is eventually redeemed by the love of a good man does not alter the passion and the guile with which she becomes the mistress of her own destiny. "'It doesn't matter,' she answered quietly, out of the darkness. "I am strong enough to suffer and live. Other girls, in my place, would have been happier – they would have suffered, and died. It doesn't matter; it will be all the same a hundred years hence . . .'"

The women are often lost in a male world. Marian Halcombe, in *The Woman in White*, had burst out with her protest. 'Men! They are the enemies of our innocence and our peace . . . they take us body and soul to themselves and fasten our helpless lives to theirs as they chain up a dog to his kennel. And what does the best of them give us in return?'

He was intent upon exploring the female sensibility in ways foreign to other Victorian novelists, and he created heroines quite unlike those of his male contemporaries. Only George Eliot, perhaps, is his superior. In his own relationship with Caroline Graves, as we have seen, he was attracted to women with a complicated and perhaps compromising past. He also enjoyed the company of independent and strong-minded women, like his mother.

It is hard, however, to see him in any contemporary sense as a feminist. He disliked the female writers of sensation novels, no doubt because they posed a challenge to him; he also seems to have had a horror of female doctors, a prejudice widely shared at the time. He was more willing to champion women as outcasts rather than to praise those who had achieved independence. He preferred the female penitent to the female professional. Yet this is not to minimise his importance in the re-creation of female character in the English novel. He was, in that sense, a pioneer.

So at the close of 1862 he had the world before him. With

The Woman in White he had achieved a sensation and with *No Name* he had managed a success. His next novel was worth £5,000. Of all the novelists in England he was the one with the brightest future. And yet, after the publication of *No Name*, the woes of Wilkie Collins were only just beginning.

12

The Chain

The ill health of the previous year did not disappear. In the early months of 1863 he was so crippled that he could not get out of bed and in so much pain that work was out of the question. It began with what he believed to be gout in the right foot that incapacitated him; he could only just hobble down the stairs. He reassured his mother by telling her that it was soothed by a poultice of cabbage leaves 'covered with oiled silk' but this was less than the truth. The gout, if such it was, then proceeded to attack the left foot as well.

The situation was not improved by a decline in the health of Caroline Graves at the same time. She had begun to suffer from some kind of nervous disease, one of those mysterious nineteenth-century complaints that admit of no easy diagnosis. His doctor, Frank Beard, was also bedridden; he had been afflicted by erysipelas, an acute skin condition that produces blisters and fevers. Is it any wonder that Collins's novels are filled with sick and ailing people? In this emergency Collins turned to John Elliotson, whom he was to describe in *The Moonstone* as 'one of the greatest of English physiologists'. Elliotson was a friend of Dickens, and was well known for his practice of mesmerism as a cure of physical and mental disorders.

Yet his theoretical prestige did not, for Collins, result in any practical benefits. Elliotson did not approve of Beard's opium treatment, and much to his patient's discomfort tried to discontinue it. He attempted to mesmerise Collins so that he might sleep without opium; he succeeded for one night, but then Collins was beset by nervous irritation and what he called 'the fidgets'. The attempts at the mesmerism of Caroline were even more deleterious; she was plunged into another nervous attack and was up all night with 'palpitations'. Collins reported that Elliotson '*has* done and *can* do nothing for me'. When Elliotson visited Harley Street Collins told him that 'I am so weak, I have no writing power left in me – give me a tonic. I must have strength.' Elliotson proposed a dose of wormwood. So Collins waited impatiently for Beard's recovery.

He was quite unable to work on the novel already bought by Smith, Elder, and was obliged to write to them in order to put off publication. Eventually the publisher allowed him to postpone delivering the first episode until the beginning of December. Collins also refused other work. He was offered the editorship of a new periodical, *Good Words*, but he declined the proposal. By the beginning of March he was starting to feel a little better; he could manage a ride in a carriage if his feet were propped up on the front seat.

In the spring of the year he decided to try a water cure on the Continent. He had already been visiting 'Dr Caplin's Electro-Chemical Bath' off Portman Square. In the *British Medical Journal* Caplin advertised his baths for 'the extraction of Mercury and other Metallic or Extraneous Substances'; Collins said that the waters worked wonders for him.

In the middle of April he and Caroline went to the spa town of Aix-la-Chapelle, where it was hoped that the medicinal water of the hot springs would bring out the 'suppressed' ailment; the mixture of sodium, chloride and hydrogen carbonate was supposed to be particularly efficacious for rheumatic diseases. He knew of a good hotel there and of an experienced doctor who could advise him on the time and length of his immersions. The water was hot, at 98 degrees, and smelled of sulphur; he was hosed down with it, and then wrapped in a very hot linen toga. He was also obliged to drink a tumbler of the spring water before breakfast; it tasted 'like the worst London egg you ever had for breakfast in your life'. But after a few days the treatment seemed to be working, and he felt himself to be stronger. After his bout in the springs, he always drove out into the surrounding hills and took short walks where the path was dry. In a letter to his mother he added that in the hotel he was continually being asked for his autograph, the requests coming from French, German and American as well as English readers. He had become a public man.

In the following month he and Caroline travelled on to the springs of Bad Wildbad in the Black Forest, where he stayed at the Hôtel de l'Ours already filled with invalids hobbling around on sticks or crutches. The water, with traces of carbonic acid, was quite different from that of Aix. It was clear and odourless, and Collins enjoyed the sensation of the hot springs bubbling up around him. He was told that twenty-four separate treatments would be sufficient, although he believed that the gout would return for one final attack before being dispersed altogether. In this belief he was mistaken. Bad Wildbad conferred one benefit on him, however. It gave him the setting for the first chapter of his next novel. Even if he was not ready to begin writing, he could at least start to plot and to plan.

On his return to England he found that he could walk more easily; he even managed to make a round trip from Harley Street to the Serpentine in Hyde Park. But he decided that a bout of sea air might improve him still further. In July he and Pigott hired a yacht at Cowes with the intention of sailing around the English coast to the Isle of Man; this also would be a setting for the new novel. But the damp air only served to irritate Collins's rheumatism further, and they abandoned the voyage at Torquay after ten days.

He was still determined to see the Isle of Man, and at the end of August he travelled with Caroline and Carrie Graves by train to Liverpool before taking a steamer to the island. The crossing was calm enough but the Isle of Man was very cold. They found apartments in a damp hotel in Douglas which materially increased the misery of Collins's rheumatism; he determined to see what he needed and then leave. By dint of much enquiry, walking and riding, he found the appropriate spot in the Calf Sound between the Calf of Man and the south-west tip of the island; it was 'wild and frightful, just what I wanted'. 'Far or near no sound was audible but the cheerless bubbling of the broken water ahead, pouring through the awful hush of silence in which earth and ocean waited for the coming day.' He then returned to his hotel, for a day or two of rest, before travelling back to London.

The hot springs and the sea air had done very little to alleviate Collins's painful condition, and so he decided to travel south to warmer climates. He now dreaded the damp English winter. He stayed in London for a little time, to 'collect my forces', but then with Caroline and Carrie he set his face towards the sunny land of Italy. He would sail from Marseilles to the port of Civitavecchia on the Tyrrhenian Sea, and from there take the train to Rome; from Rome the little party would go on to Naples.

Before he left for Italy, however, he arranged to keep his name before the public with the two volumes entitled *My Miscellanies*. These were essentially articles taken from *Household Words* and *All the Year Round*, from the account of his lodgings in London and Paris to his examination of 'The Unknown Public'.

And so on to Italy. The Collins family, if they can so be called, rested in Paris for a week before travelling to Marseilles. They were supposed to take the sea-crossing to Genoa but the weather prevented them; so they travelled by *vettura* or four-wheeled carriage. Their route took them along the coast from Nice to San Remo before proceeding to Genoa itself. Already he felt the blessings of the warm air and of the cloudless sky, of the palm trees and the lemon groves. He was now able to walk up the hills with a firm step and felt infinitely better. From Genoa they took the steamer to Livorno, the port 10 miles from Pisa. When they arrived at Pisa they were greeted by a sirocco which proved torture to Collins, 'and the pangs of Sciatica wrung me in both *hams* at once'. A sea journey at night to Civitavecchia also proved a misery for Caroline and Harriet, who both became violently seasick. But a two-hour train journey took them to Rome, where they found a good first-floor apartment of five rooms. But the weather was against him; he was preoccupied with it, because his health and well-being depended upon it. He was greeted with rain, thunder and a cold north-east wind. He had become a complete valetudinarian, driven out of public places by the pervading dampness, shutting the windows against the chill and then opening them again to get some air. He did not intend to stay in the capital for long, however, and instead wished to make Naples his home for the season.

By the middle of November they had arrived. Once more he was confronted by rain, a driving and tropical rain that obscured the sea and Vesuvius. He was tormented by hail and lightning, deafened by thunder, and narrowly missed a hurricane. When the rain abated it was succeeded by a hot and damp sirocco wind. These were not the ideal conditions for a rheumatic invalid. He visited the remnants of the English community whom he had met in the past, and noted that Naples had not changed very much in the interim. Urchins and deformed beggars and vagabond cabmen still occupied the streets; the fruit stalls and iced-water stalls stood on every corner; the inhabitants of Naples still conversed in shrieks and wild gestures, and the old smells of the city still lingered.

Now he decided that the climate was too 'relaxing' for him; even the warmth was enervating, doing him more harm than good. His appetite was failing, and his foot was more painful. He was becoming exhausted and depressed. He decided to move on to Florence by way of Rome, but when he finally reached the capital at the beginning of December, he decided to stay. The dry, cold air did him good. He could walk for two hours at a stretch in the crisp atmosphere, with the north wind acting as a restorative. He remained here for three months.

In Italy his imagination was quickened. He had great hopes for an entirely new and different novel, and the ideas for it came to him in swarms. He wrote them down and then considered them in every light, but already the outline of the plot was clear to him. He knew what the ending would be. In Rome – on 8 January 1864 – he celebrated his fortieth birthday. But, as he said, 'I don't *feel* old.' He had no respectable prejudices or regular habits; he did not sleep after dinner or avoid public amusements. In Rome, for example, he was going to the opera all the time. Yet in later years his contemporaries would notice that he seemed, and looked, older than he actually was.

They returned to London in March after an absence of four months. It was only now that Collins could properly work upon the new novel. At first he made only slow and hesitant progress; he had abstained from literary practice for a year and a half and, as he told his mother, 'it is not wonderful that my hand should be out'. Yet at least he had made a start. So he made reasonable progress through the spring and early summer, gathering strength and confidence as he went along. The monthly numbers of the *Cornhill* offered an alternative to the more insistent weekly dead-lines of *All the Year Round*, but Collins was still determined to keep at least three months ahead of the printer. He was also pleased to discover that he could write less; one monthly episode was equivalent only to two of the previous weekly episodes. His writing demands were thereby cut by a half.

He was a little distracted by the circumambient noise of Harley Street. Like many London streets it was festooned with musicians and assorted entertainments, including organs and bagpipes and bands. He contemplated a move to the more sedate and secluded neighbourhood of the Temple, but nothing transpired. In June he was able to submit the first part of the manuscript to George Smith; the first chapter, 'The Travellers', is set at the baths in Bad Wildbad he had so recently attended. It was the beginning of *Armadale*, one of the most dramatic and convoluted of all Collins's narratives.

He wished to shift the setting to Norfolk, and so in August he took the train to Great Yarmouth; with his companions, Edward Pigott and Charles Ward, he also indulged in a little light sailing off the Norfolk coast. He inspected the Norfolk Broads, too, where 'the shore lay clear and low in the sunshine, fringed darkly at certain points by rows of dwarf trees; and dotted here and there, in the opener spaces, with windmills and reed-thatched cottages, of puddled mud . . . while to the east a long, gently undulating line of reeds followed the windings of the Broad, and shut out all view of the watery wastes beyond'. This was Horsey Mere, a broad swept by the wind from the North Sea, which in the novel becomes Hurle Mere.

And then once more he succumbed to illness. He seemed to believe that he had been attacked by gout of the brain. 'My mind is perfectly clear,' he told Pigott in September, 'but the nervous misery I suffer is indescribable.' He was not sure if he would be able to continue with the novel, a delay that in itself would be a disaster. Beard himself could not decide when he would be able to work again. There is no such thing as gout of the brain, and it seems to be shorthand for severe mental anxiety. The 'misery' of the nerves may have been further exacerbated by an over-liberal use of opium.

Yet the disaster was averted and the spell of nervous tension had abated by the following month. His mood was further lightened by the favourable response to the early chapters. Dickens's sister-in-law, Georgina Hogarth, could not sleep until she had finished them and Collins reported to Charles Ward that 'the *Printers* are highly interested in the story . . . it is no easy matter to please the printers'.

Armadale began its public life in the November issue of the *Cornhill* and, even as he continued work on the subsequent episodes, he once more became anxious and ill at ease; a specialist in nervous diseases, Charles Radcliffe, diagnosed the problem as one of 'gouty irritation' and prescribed a regimen of exercise accompanied by a light diet. His essential purpose, like that of most doctors, was to reassure the patient. Nothing seriously wrong with you. No reason for any alarm about your work.

Charles Collins gave what was probably the more accurate diagnosis in calling it a case of inherited 'Collinsian nerves'. He drew upon his own experiences to illuminate those of his brother. 'When you are doing nothing you are pretty well but directly that you begin to work again . . . think you suffer.' He added that 'to think about work at all, especially at moments of compelled inaction, as in bed for instance, is highly dangerous'. So the Collins brothers may both have been prey to night terrors. Beard gave him a cordial made up of quinine, acid and dandelion that seemed to help.

His general nervousness could not have been improved by a move of house at the same time. A few days before Christmas he and Caroline took up residence at 9 Melcombe Place, Dorset Square; it was approximately a quarter of a mile from Harley Street, on the other side of the New Road. Any pretence at marriage was dropped, and Caroline Graves appears both in the rate books and in the London street directories. Her name also now appears in Collins's bank account at Coutts.

The work on *Armadale* was relentless, and he only managed short interruptions. He travelled to Paris for a week at the end of February 1865, where he spent much of the time at the theatre. He visited his mother in Tunbridge Wells. He went up to Great Yarmouth with Edward Pigott for the sailing. He took the chair at the twentieth anniversary festival of the Royal General

Theatrical Fund, when at the end of almost every sentence he was applauded.

He visited Dickens at Gad's Hill Place, where a fellow guest described how 'poor Wilkie Collins who needs rest used to sneak off to the library and go to sleep with a cigar. Dickens pried him out and said, "None of this. No smoking in the library in the daytime – you must work at something."' In a game of charades Dickens appeared with a black handkerchief on his head and a fire shovel in his hand to mimic the beheading of Charles I; Collins played the royal victim.

Frederick Lehmann gives a curious report of an evening party in London during this period. He noted that 'the Dickens and Collins faction' were at a different end of the drawing room from 'Society'. The reason was clear enough. Collins was living with his mistress at Melcombe Place while Dickens had divorced his wife in favour of an actress. The two novelists, despite their fame and success, were not quite respectable.

Collins finally completed *Armadale* in the spring of 1866, and he told his mother that he had never before been so moved and excited by any of his endings. He celebrated the event by going to Paris with Frederick Lehmann for a week and, in the warm weather, he was happy to be simply idle. He had discharged what he considered to be 'heavy responsibility' in the face of great difficulties; he had come through.

It was published in two volumes by Smith, Elder at the end of May. It is the longest novel that Collins ever wrote, and the plot is too detailed to be amenable to précis. You cannot turn a labyrinth into a straight path. The narrative moves in setting from the Norfolk Broads to Borough High Street, from Germany to the Isle of Man, from Madeira to Naples, from an abortionist's clinic in Pimlico to a country house in Somerset; the incidents vary from a murder at sea to an attempted murder by poison gas. It begins with a deathbed confession of murder and ends with a suicide. It concerns two young men with the same name, a recurrent dream of fatality and terror, and a detective mystery. It is perhaps too full of incident to be finally satisfying, and by the end the reader has supped full of sensation. Yet T. S. Eliot remarked that it 'has no merit beyond melodrama, and it has every merit that melodrama can have'.

It is chiefly remarkable for its female protagonist, Miss Gwilt, a consummate intriguer and adventuress who inveigles her way into the heart of one of the young men. 'Should I be wrong . . . if I guessed that you have something on your mind – something which neither my tea nor my talk can charm away? Are men as curious as women? Is the something – Me?' She has been in turn a forger, a murderer, a thief, and a bigamist. One of her associates is Mrs Oldershaw who, after peddling quack medicines, becomes the proprietress of the Ladies' Toilette Repository, an establishment that is essentially a backstreet abortion clinic. She is a character rich in comic possibilities that Collins unfailingly exploits. Here is her advice to Lydia Gwilt. 'You shall have the sleeping drops tomorrow. In the meantime, I say at the end what I said at the beginning – no recklessness. Don't encourage poetical feelings by looking at the stars; and don't talk about the night being awfully quiet. There are people (in observatories) paid to look at the stars for you; leave it to them.'

The climactic scene is set in a sanatorium on Hampstead Heath, where Mrs Midwinter (aka Miss Gwilt) is about to administer poison gas to her husband's closest friend, thus completing the air of vivid and almost hysterical melodrama that accompanies the complicated plot in which characters overhear secrets or lurk beneath opened windows. It is all a great adventure with Collins himself pulling the strings – gently here, tightly there, loosely somewhere else. He acts as a dispassionate observer; he sets the scene; he carefully describes the rooms in which the action is to take place; he introduces the characters one by one.

And there is a moment which anticipates the actions of a later detective, Lieutenant Colombo. It is given the name of 'Pedgift's postscript' when 'the lawyer suddenly checked his exit at the opened door; came back softly to his chair, with his pinch of snuff suspended between his box and his nose; said "By-the-by, there's a point occurs to me"'.

The novel, to use Collins's own words in another context, is 'held together by some mysterious connection, and was tending to some unimaginable end'. 'I was wondering,' one character says, 'if there is such a thing as chance.' But the world is not ruled by chance; it is ruled by fatality. The characters of this world come together by ones and twos, converging from widely different quarters, drawing slowly together in a sphere 'which was soon destined to assemble them all, for the first and the last time in this world, face to face'. In *Basil*, for example, the villain becomes 'the bearer of a curse that shall follow you' and 'the instrument of a fatality pronounced against you long ere we met'.

The critics of *Armadale* were not uniformly respectful. The *Spectator* described its anti-heroine, Miss Gwilt, as 'fouler than the refuse of the streets'. The Collins world 'is peopled by a set of scoundrels qualified by a set of fools, and watched by retributive justice in the shape of attorneys and spies'. The reviewer in the *Athenaeum* complained that his characters 'may live and breathe in "the sinks and sewers" of society' but they should not be displayed in fiction.

A more allusive note was struck by a critic in the *Saturday Review* who noticed the 'galvanic power' of Collins's narrative and remarked that the characters are kept in motion by 'the sheer force and energy of the author's will'. In a period when the powers of mesmerism were being explored and applied for a variety of purposes, the idea of the novelist as mesmerist is significant. An account of *No Name* had remarked that 'from the beginning of the first chapter of his work, he keeps his eye steadily fixed on the last. So long as you have his book open, you are spell-bound . . . the book enchains you, but you detest it while it enchains.' The 'chain', as we have observed, is one of the key metaphors of Collins's fiction – the chain of events, the chain of connections, the chain binding the reader to the tale. This mesmeric power can be associated with Collins's interest in clairvoyance and animal magnetism together with the other hidden powers of the mind. The workings of 'Destiny' may come in different forms.

13

The Stone

George Smith never did recoup the £5,000 he had offered Collins
for the manuscript of *Armadale*; after some initial enthusiasm,
sales were slow. Yet Collins refused to be downhearted and at a
later date told one correspondent that he considered it to be the
best novel he had ever written. Then he went yachting once more
with Edward Pigott with the help of a steady breeze and a smooth
sea.

It may have been on this short vacation that he and Pigott
decided to make an extended journey to Italy. Before he left,
however, he had accepted a proposal for the revival of *The Frozen
Deep* by a professional company at the Olympic. Since it was
imperative to leave for Italy on the date they had set, Collins was
in a frantic rush of business made all the more wearying by a bad
cold. Originally the play had been scheduled for the Christmas
season but the failure of another production brought it forward
to October. He read the play to the cast and even supervised the
early rehearsals. He had hoped to use the original sets, but they
had all been cut apart. He broke off to visit his mother at Tunbridge
Wells and then hurried back to the theatre to sketch the playbill
and talk to the manager.

Then he was off to Italy. He managed to spend a day in Paris
where he spoke to the manager of the Théâtre Français, François
Regnier, about a production of *Armadale*. He and Pigott then
travelled through Switzerland to Milan and Rome; Pigott was now
the chief reporter on foreign affairs for the *Daily News*, and he
wanted the opportunity to see for himself the complications of

Italian politics at the time when the Venetian republic was about to be absorbed by the recently created kingdom of Italy. Collins's own visit, however, was curtailed when he received a letter from his French collaborator on the play of *Armadale* who needed urgent advice. On the same day a letter also arrived from London which gave him the unwelcome news that *The Frozen Deep* had not been a success at the Olympic; the audience on the opening night had been enthusiastic enough, but ticket sales had not been high. The play was considered 'slow', and perhaps a little old-fashioned for a modern public. The *London Review* had described the characters as 'mere sketches', and the costumes as 'unnatural and ridiculous'.

So he travelled to Paris as quickly as possible, where he sorted out the problems of the collaborator, before going on to London for discussions with Horace Wigan of the Olympic. In truth *The Frozen Deep* was never going to be a success, and it was taken off after a 'run' of six weeks. It was said that there had even been hisses from the audience at some of the performances. Collins told one of the actresses that it had all been 'disastrous'. A few months later, too, Collins was told by Regnier that *Armadale* could not be produced on the French stage. Collins had harboured hopes for its production in London, too, but it was never performed there in its original form.

Collins had great expectations of the theatre. He believed that he could make a fortune by it, in London and in Paris, and he always said that his creative gift was essentially a theatrical one. Soon enough he was planning his narratives with eventual stage production in mind, in effect turning them into quintessentially theatrical novels. On a personal rather than a professional level, many of his friends were actors; he had a taste for green-room gossip, and he enjoyed the company of men and women who were immune to many of the Victorian pieties. He even harboured the ambition of becoming a theatrical manager.

His own taste in drama was wide enough, with a particular

attention to the French theatre of Dumas and of Scribe. In England he was less hopeful and respectful, considering most English acting to be third-rate and the English public to be imbecilic. Nevertheless he tried repeatedly for success, and at one stage of his career three of his plays were performed in the West End within a space of eighteen months. He had a preference for melodrama in a period when, according to one observer, theatrical success relied upon 'the most prodigious excitement, the most appalling catastrophes, the most harrowing situations'. His own practice is reflected in his tribute to the actor Charles Fechter, when he declared that 'an audience cannot be excited without being thrilled. It cannot be thrilled without being made to feel . . .'

At the beginning of 1867, undeterred by the relative financial failure of *Armadale*, he found a fresh source of optimism. He wanted to discover a new public, and had decided that he would begin to write for the penny journals. He was bursting with ideas for new books and new plays. He even conceived a scheme for combining the plots of *The Lighthouse*, *The Frozen Deep* and *The Red Vial* into one novel for the penny public; it is probably just as well that he never managed to achieve this feat.

But he did soon have the notion of a new and thoroughly original novel. By the spring he was negotiating terms with *All the Year Round* for its appearance in weekly numbers. He had clearly decided that the penny public was not yet ready for him. He took the first three parts with him to Gad's Hill Place in the summer and, when he read them aloud, Dickens was much taken by the plot. Dickens told Wills that 'it is a very curious story, wild and yet domestic', and he believed that 'it is in many respects much better than anything he has done'. Two weeks later Collins reported to his mother that he was 'in a whirl of work'. Collins had planned to make the new novel much shorter than *Armadale*, and although it ran longer than he intended, it was still only three-quarters of the length of its predecessor.

He did much of his research for the novel in the library of the Athenaeum; it was one of the London clubs which he frequented. There he consulted volumes on the Hindu religion and on Indian lore. He read C. W. King's *The Natural History of Precious Stones and of the Precious Metals* and Talboys Wheeler's various accounts of India. He met Englishmen who had travelled to, or lived in, India. He was about to call this novel *The Serpent's Eye*, until he hit upon the more suggestive title of *The Moonstone*.

In the summer Collins moved house once more to 90 Gloucester Place, Portman Square. He was beset by difficulties with the builders, and the general upheaval of repairs and alterations; at one point he had to take refuge with the Lehmanns in Highgate in order to work undisturbed. He signed a twenty-year lease for the property, which suggests that he had the definite intention of taking root; in fact he stayed in the house, with Caroline Graves, for most of the rest of his life. It was a terraced house on five floors, built at the beginning of the nineteenth century; the dining room and sitting room were on the ground floor, while Collins's study was on the first floor overlooking the street. The study was originally a double drawing room, and was spacious; it was, for him, the heart of the house. Caroline Graves had her own bedroom. His bedroom seems to have been at the top of the house, perhaps to escape the noise of the street. The rooms were in general large and airy and, for Collins, Gloucester Place had the inestimable benefit of being located on dry soil. He fled from damp.

He leased out the stables in the mews behind Gloucester Place, although he had difficulties with the tenant. The household was completed by three servants, generally two women and a man or boy, and by a dog. Tommy was a Scottish terrier of voracious appetite but gentle manners. It might be described as a large and comfortable London house, with the oddity that Collins refused to have gas. The house is now numbered 65 Gloucester Place, and has a blue plaque to Wilkie Collins to one side of the door.

The present author has spent many pleasant evenings there in the company of a friend who rented the third floor in what is now a house of flats.

The pressure of work was now compounded by the time spent with Dickens upon their first Christmas collaboration for seven years. 'No Thoroughfare' was written principally in the Swiss chalet that Dickens had erected at the bottom of his garden at Gad's Hill Place. The two novelists planned it as a drama as well as a story, and as a result it is divided into an 'Overture' and four 'Acts'. It has to do with a foundling who has been given the wrong name, with all the possible misfortunes that might arise from mistaken identity; there is an attempt at murder on the Simplon Pass, and the villain dies in an avalanche. True love prevails. It has all the ingredients that Dickens wished, including 'ghostly interest, picturesque interest, breathless interest of time and circumstance'. These were the conditions for pleasing the Victorian public. They finished the fourth act working side by side in Dickens's bedroom, moving ineluctably towards the climactic scene. The end of the third act sets the tone for what follows.

Obenreizer: I am the thief and the forger. In a minute more,
   I shall take the proof from your dead body!
Vendale (*confusedly; feeling the influence of the laudanum*):
   You villain! What have I done to you?

Dickens was already making urgent preparation for his reading tour of America, and so left much of the final dramatisation of the story to Collins. The play itself was long, at a length of some four hours, but the audiences were enthusiastic; it ran at the Adelphi in the Strand for 151 performances before transferring to the Standard Theatre in Shoreditch where it remained until the summer of 1868. It was Collins's first great success upon the London stage. Dickens believed that it was too long and that it dragged a little. Collins had a habit of explaining everything to the audience, sometimes more than once; the interruptions naturally impeded the dramatic action.

Yet the play was immensely benefited by the presence of Charles Fechter, a French actor who became a close friend of both Dickens and Collins. He had helped to assist in the dramatic adaptation and, in Collins's words, 'fell madly in love with the subject'. He assumed the part of Obenreizer, the villain, and according to Collins played the role in every moment of his waking life. He was Obenreizer in the morning and Obenreizer at the dinner table. He was the champion of what might be called French naturalism; he spoke, rather than delivered, his lines.

After their work together Collins and Fechter became close friends. Collins recalled later that

> Fechter's lively mind was, to use his own expression, 'full of plots'. He undertook to tell me stories enough for all the future novels and plays that I could possibly live to write. His power of invention was unquestionably remarkable; but his method of narration was so confused that it was not easy to follow him, and his respect for those terrible obstacles in the way of free imagination known as probabilities was, to say the least of it, in some need of improvement.

He was always heavily in debt, and was inclined to borrow from one friend in order to pay another.

With Fechter, too, Collins shared a passion for food. The actor had his own cook, whom Collins described as 'one of the finest artists that ever handled a saucepan'. Fechter once persuaded her to create a potato dinner in six courses and an egg dinner in eight courses. Collins also had decided tastes. He disliked the stolid Victorian diet of boiled pork and greens and pease pudding, of mutton and stewed beef and parsnips and carrots. In *A Rogue's*

Life he depicts with horror a dinner of 'gravy soup, turbot and lobster-sauce, haunch of mutton, boiled fowls and tongue, lukewarm oyster patties and sticky curry for side-dishes; wild duck, cabinet-pudding, jelly, cream and tartlets'. At this late date it sounds exotic but, as Collins notes, not when you have to eat it every day. In a late novel, *Blind Love*, a landlady provides food 'cooked to a degree of imperfection only attained in an English kitchen'.

His idea of perfection was French cooking, and he once described meat as simply 'a material for sauces'. He adored black pepper and garlic; on one occasion he applied so much garlic to a pie that he was obliged to take to his bed with a gastric attack. He sometimes gorged himself on pâté de foie gras, and had a passion for eating steamed asparagus cold with salad oil. In France he dined on oysters and Chablis, and on omelettes garnished with radishes. He hated the flummery of formal dinners, however. In his own invitations he would add 'without ceremony as usual', or would put 'no company' and 'no dress'.

With wine, too, he was something of a connoisseur. His drink of choice was the driest possible champagne. 'Isn't a pint of champagne nice drinking, this hot weather,' one of his characters remarks. 'Just cooled with ice . . . and poured, fizzing, into a silver mug. Lord, how delicious!' He also professed to believe, like many others, that champagne was 'good' for the health, but he also drank burgundy and hock and Moselle. He had great faith in the restorative powers of tobacco, too, which revived and calmed him. He relished cigars, and felt nothing but pity for those who did not smoke. He also took snuff incessantly.

After Collins had 'seen off' Dickens on his American tour, at a grand banquet in the Freemasons' Hall that Caroline and Carrie Graves also attended, he returned to his desk at Gloucester Place in order to continue work on *The Moonstone*. The first episode of the novel was published in *All the Year Round* at the beginning of 1868, and the omens for a prodigious success were already visible. Soon enough the crowds assembled outside the offices of the periodical on publication day.

Two weeks after first publication, however, he received the unwelcome news that Harriet Collins was seriously ill. She had the familial complaint of nervous prostration, but now it had taken the alarming form of complete breakdown of her faculties. He went down to her country cottage, but nervous complications of his own brought him back to London where he summoned Frank Beard. He said that he had been 'struck prostrate' and was 'crippled in every limb'; but the principal agony was reserved for his eyes that were so inflamed he could neither read nor write.

He confessed that he had been obliged to dictate the novel from his bed 'in the intervals of grief, in the intermissions of pain'. He was exaggerating a little, since only five pages of the manuscript are in the hand of Carrie Graves, but there is no doubt that this period represented one of the great trials of his life. He had always been close to his mother, and when her death came in the middle of February he was so overcome with grief that he could not attend her funeral. The gout in the eyes might have prevented his attendance, in any case, but the pain of the occasion would have been too great. He said that her death was the 'bitterest affliction of my life' and fifteen years later he told a correspondent that 'when I think of her, I still know what heartache means'.

Yet, in a preface to a revised edition of the novel, he wrote that his painful labours on *The Moonstone* were for him a 'blessed relief' from his mental agony. 'I doubt', he wrote, 'I should have lived to write another book, if the responsibility of the weekly publication of this story had not forced me to rally my sinking energies of body and mind – to dry my useless tears, and to conquer my merciless pains.'

The amount of laudanum he took, while writing the narrative

in these distressing circumstances, was considerable. He professed to have no memory of much of the plot. 'I was not only pleased and astonished at the finale,' he is supposed to have said, 'but did not recognise it as my own.' It is ironic, perhaps, that the plot of the novel itself devolves upon the erasure of memory by the use of opium. But the laudanum did not otherwise affect his faculties; the narrative remains sharp and detailed.

The death of Harriet Collins might have meant that, in theory, Caroline Graves could come into the open. It was his mother's disapproval that had previously required his circumspection and secrecy on the matter of their relationship. He put the situation delicately in a later novel, *The Evil Genius*:

'Free to marry if you like?' she persisted.

He said 'Yes' once more – and kept his face steadily turned away from her. She waited a while. He neither moved nor spoke.

Surviving the slow death little by little of all her other illusions, one last hope had lingered in her heart. It was killed by that cruel look, fixed on the view of the street.

'I'll try to think of a place that we can go to at the seaside.' Having said these words she slowly moved away to the door . . .

This is of course a fictional conversation, and may not be related to any actual scene. Yet it is suggestive. In any case a further obstacle arose between Collins and Caroline Graves in the shape of another woman.

In the year of Harriet Collins's death Martha Rudd emerges by Collins's side. It had previously been thought that, as a native of Norfolk, Collins had discovered her on one of his excursions to that region. She was a daughter of a shepherd. Yet a very well-informed obituary, after Collins's death, states that Martha Rudd had been one of Harriet Collins's servants. She 'was a housemaid in the employ of Wilkie Collins's mother and was very devoted to her while she lived'. The timing of her appearance, therefore, makes perfect sense. He may have seduced her while she was in his mother's employment, or he may have taken the opportunity of Harriet's death to bring her to London.

Martha Rudd, given the name of Mrs Dawson, had been placed in lodgings in 33 Bolsover Street, a ten- or fifteen-minute walk away from Gloucester Place. This was the street in which Collins's grandfather had once had a picture-dealing business. She was now twenty-three years old, while he was forty-four. Even though she was to bear him three children, she is only ever directly mentioned by Collins in his correspondence with his solicitor. To his closest acquaintance she was described as his 'morganatic marriage'; a morganatic marriage is one contracted between persons of unequal rank. It is possible that he never introduced her to Caroline Graves, and it is unlikely that he ever took her among his friends. He was, perhaps. a little ashamed of her. But he needed her society and her bed; she remained with him until the end of his life.

Another Victorian, Arthur Munby, loved to penetrate the class barriers of Victorian society with his obsession for working-class women. He fell in love with a 'robust hardworking peasant lass, with the marks of labour and servitude upon her everywhere', for example, and he was enamoured of many others. Collins may have had a similar taste.

The Moonstone ran for thirty-two episodes, or eight months, in *All the Year Round*. In the month before the final episode appeared, the novel was published in volume form by the Tinsley Brothers. One of their employees in their office at Catherine Street said later that 'Wilkie's solicitors sent in a draft which was a regular corker; it would pretty well cover the gable of an ordinary sized house'.

The Moonstone has held its place as one of Collins's most successful and popular novels. In the course of the narrative eleven different narrators give their accounts of the theft of a magnificent jewel from a country house. It is on one level the paradigm of the detective story. The detective, Sergeant Cuff, is an eccentric whose principal passion is for the cultivation of roses; he is also one of the first fictional characters to employ a magnifying glass. Other aspects of traditional detective fiction also appear here. The members of the country-house party can all in turn be considered suspects. The perpetrator of the crime is in fact the least likely of them all. The astute detective is contrasted with a bumbling and inefficient local police force, but in the end an amateur solves the crime that has baffled all the professionals. The blame shifts from person to person in an apparently endless game of pass the parcel while the whole complex affair is eventually resolved by a dramatic reconstruction of the events of the fatal night. In all these aspects *The Moonstone* can be see to be the true source and spring of the English detective mystery.

Criminology was in its infancy when Collins wrote *The Moonstone*, but the idea of the detective had already caught the public imagination at a time when it was believed that the incidence of crime was rising. Collins himself coined the phrase 'detective *fever*'. The detective was the official meant to restore order to a chaotic world; he was the secret policeman who would be able to infiltrate the groups or societies poised to create terror in the streets. An essay in *Chambers's Journal* of 1843 notes that 'at times the detective policeman attires himself in the dress of ordinary individuals'. The detective became the symbol of urban anonymity and a symptom of the new interest in the professional expert. In *The Moonstone* he is supposed to resolve the issues and to remove all the fear or neurosis that has attended them; his role is to re-establish the old and familiar patterns of existence.

The multiple narratives of the novel lend substance to the

unending suspense. As one character says, 'from all I can see, one interpretation is just as likely to be right as the other'. Nothing is what it seems. 'I saw the pony harnessed myself. In the infernal network of mysteries and uncertainties that now surrounded us, I declare it was a relief to observe how well the buckles and straps understood each other!' Collins counsels us to wait for the buckles and straps of the plot to be fastened together at the end.

Yet it is more than a mystery. The moonstone itself is a piece of sacred Indian theatre, and a group of Indians come to England in order to recover it. In the wake of the Indian Mutiny it was common enough to portray them as bloodthirsty savages, but Collins takes them and their religion seriously. They, too, have been wronged; the stone was in fact originally stolen by an English soldier, grown drunk on rapine and riot, who brought it home with him. It was part of his imperial legacy.

When the stone is later stolen from a young woman's bedroom at night, the theft becomes a symbol of rape, which might be construed as the rape of India. The house steward, Mr Betteredge, sums up the bewilderment which is then engendered in a 'right-thinking' Englishman. 'Here was our quiet English house suddenly invaded by a devilish Indian diamond – bringing after it a conspiracy of living rogues, set loose on us by the vengeance of a dead man . . . Whoever heard the like of it – in the nineteenth century, mind; in an age of progress, and in a country which rejoices in the blessings of the British constitution?' At the end of the novel it is returned to its rightful place in the city of Somnauth.

If Collins states the grievances of the Indians, he also draws attention to the plight of the English lower class. 'Ha, Mr Betteredge,' one poor girl says, 'the day is not far off when the poor will rise against the rich. I pray Heaven they may begin with *him*.' Betteredge himself reflects on the differences between the high life and the low life. 'Necessity, which spares our betters, has no pity on *us*.' Collins was always aware of the shadows that

Victorian civilisation cast, and there is not one novel that does not on one level or another draw attention to the poor and the outcast.

Collins waited with apprehension for the response. 'I awaited its reception by the public,' he wrote later, 'with an eagerness of anxiety I have never felt before or since.' He believed that *The Moonstone* was the best novel he had ever written with a stronger degree of 'popularity' in it than in any of his books since *The Woman in White*. In this judgement he was proved correct. William Tinsley recorded that

> there were scenes in Wellington Street that doubtless did the author's and publisher's hearts good. And especially when the serial was nearing its ending, on publishing days there would be quite a crowd of anxious readers waiting for the new number . . . Even the porters and boys were interested in the story, and read the new number in sly corners, and often with their packs on their backs . . .

Bets were placed on how, and where, the jewel would be recovered. There had been nothing quite like it since *The Woman in White*.

The first edition of 1,500 novels sold out quickly enough, and a second edition of 500 copies was printed. Robert Louis Stevenson, at the age of seventeen, wrote to his mother that '*The Moonstone* is frightfully interesting; isn't the detective prime?' Despite his initial enthusiasm for the book, Dickens's admiration did not last. 'I quite agree with you about The Moonstone,' he told W. H. Wills. 'The construction is wearisome beyond endurance, and there is a vein of obstinate conceit in it that makes enemies of readers.' His dislike, however, did not prevent him from adopting it as one of the models for *The Mystery of Edwin Drood*.

The reviewers were not enthusiastic. Praise was once more afforded for its ingenuity of construction. One contemporary critic noticed that 'not a window is opened, a door shut, or a nose blown, but, depend upon it, the act will have something to do with the end of the book'. Yet some reviewers believed that it was ingenuity and nothing more. The critic of the *Pall Mall Gazette* wrote that 'in sliding panels, trap doors and artificial beards, Mr Collins is nearly as clever as anyone who ever fried a pancake in a hat'. It was true enough, as the reviewers said, that Collins could not create 'characters' in the familiar sense. They do not, for example, have the overflowing energy and vitality of even Dickens's minor characters. They act as if they are on an invisible stage; they are a bundle of striking attributes or a repertoire of effects. They are not fundamentally real; they do not live or grow one with another. Yet they are entirely appropriate for the kind of novel that Collins wished to write. You cannot expect a novelist to work against his natural grain.

It was believed that the 'detective element' disqualified the novel as a work of art, when in fact it opened the way for an entirely new direction in English literature. There had been earlier exercises in the genre, but all of them are inconsiderable beside the over-whelming power and authority of *The Moonstone*. Collins's novel, since its publication in 1868, has never been out of print.

14

A Change of Heart

At the end of his painful labours on *The Moonstone* Collins planned a journey to Switzerland in the company of Frederick Lehmann. He was staying with him in July 1868, in Highgate, and they decided to travel on together to St Moritz. 'I *must* get away,' he said. So they took the Antwerp steamer at the beginning of August; at St Moritz Collins enjoyed the enchanting scenery and was enlivened by the mountain air, touched as it was by the breath of the glaciers and the scent of the pine woods. He would go on to Baden-Baden and then, at the beginning of September, return home.

Yet home was not quite the same place as before, since the presence of Martha Rudd in his life had already provoked new complications. At some stage of this year Caroline Graves left Gloucester Place and, on 29 October, married Joseph Charles Clow at Marylebone's parish church. It would seem that the arrival of Martha at Bolsover Street, and Collins's refusal to marry her, had pushed Caroline into another alliance.

On the day of the wedding Dickens wrote to his sister-in-law that 'for anything one knows, the whole matrimonial pretence may be a lie of that woman's, intended to make him marry her'. So it seems that, at the very least, Collins had come under a great deal of pressure. It was not unreasonable for Caroline Graves to seek the legal and social safety of a marriage. It may not have been a wholly amicable separation but it was one that had been agreed between the parties. Collins was present at the ceremony, and one of the witnesses was Frank Beard. Rendered more financially secure, after the will of his mother had been read, Collins may also have given her money.

Very little is known of Clow himself. He signed himself as 'gentleman' on the marriage certificate. He was a man of twenty-seven, the son of a distiller; since another relative was an ale merchant, it is possible that Clow was also in the drinks trade. It is not known where the newly married couple lived. They may perhaps have removed to his parents' house on Avenue Road, overlooking Regent's Park. Carrie Graves stayed with Collins at Gloucester Place, as did Caroline Graves's mother-in-law, Frances Clow. Carrie, who had just left school, was to stay on for the next ten years, becoming his amanuensis as well as his companion, until the time of her own marriage. A further change lay ahead. By the late autumn of the year Martha Rudd knew herself to be pregnant with Collins's first child.

In the spring of 1869 he spoke of the 'anxieties' and 'troubles' that were attacking him. These no doubt concerned his unusual domestic arrangements, and he always said that the most debilitating anxieties came from distress 'at home'. Could it be that he was distressed at the imminent birth of an illegitimate child? And could he redeem the situation by marrying Martha?

But his troubles may have also been in part related to his declining health. He had started a new treatment to ameliorate the effects of gout without the indiscriminate use of laudanum; he told Frederick Lehmann's sister that he was 'stabbed every night at ten with a sharp-pointed syringe which injects morphia under my skin'. It was hoped that the dose could be slowly lowered until he could refrain from opium altogether; this was not, however, the result. By the following month he was wracked with pain, and could only write by shifting the pen from his left hand to his right hand.

His mood was not lightened by the failure of his next play, *Black and White*, that opened at the Adelphi at the end of March.

Charles Fechter had come up with the idea of what was billed as a love story in three acts. Set in Trinidad in 1830 it concerns the fate of a 'mixed race' suitor for a white lady's hand; he is first of all bought and sold as a slave but then, by legal technicality, becomes once more free and available. Exit the happy lovers.

Miss M: I live again. You are free! (*takes Leyrac's hand*)
Leyrac: No! (*kisses her hand*) I am your slave! (*Picture*)

The omens were not propitious. Fechter became ill during the rehearsals and Collins himself caught a cold from the stage draughts during the daytime. Yet the first night was successful enough and Collins was brought before the audience to accept its applause. The drama is of no great merit and, although it ran at the Adelphi for sixty nights, it often played to almost empty houses, and the provincial 'run' was no more successful. One review mentioned 'the breathless rapidity with which the most conflicting events succeed one another'; but this was always Collins's style. He himself blamed the failure on the surfeit of theatrical productions of *Uncle Tom's Cabin*; they had no connection with each other but the shared theme of slavery was enough to deter the public.

Yet Collins was never a writer who succumbed to disappointment, and soon enough he was beginning to 'lay the keel' of another novel. At a time when marriage, or the possibility of marriage, was much on his mind he began to enquire into the state of the matrimonial laws. He was generally incensed by the fact that a woman had no right to control her property after marriage; in the words of Blackstone 'the very being or legal existence of a woman is suspended'. So he began work on *Man and Wife*. 'Yours is a common case', a woman is told in the novel. 'In the present state of the law I can do nothing for you . . . you are a married woman. The law doesn't allow a married woman to call anything her own

. . . Your husband has a right to sell your furniture if he likes. I am sorry for you; I can't hinder him.' The wife is in effect another form of property to be exploited. Even as Collins was writing his new novel the Members of Parliament were debating what became the first Married Women's Property Act of 1870, which offered only limited redress to the aggrieved woman. An article for *Fraser's Magazine*, in 1868, had the title 'Criminals, Idiots, Women and Minors: Is the Classification Sound?'.

In particular Collins took exception to the Scottish laws of marriage. By a practice known as 'irregular marriage' a man and woman could be pronounced husband and wife without the need for any formal ceremony or declaration. If, for example, they spent the night in a hotel or in an inn, they were deemed to have consented to the union. A letter of intent, from one to the other, was enough to constitute a legal marriage. He quoted a contemporaneous judgment that 'Consent makes marriage. No form of ceremony, civil or religious; no notice before, or publication after; no cohabitation, no writing, no witnesses even, are essential to the constitution of this, the most important contract which two persons can enter into.' This was the pivot upon which his novel was based.

He did his research in other areas, also, and was asking a friend for advice on physical sports; he was intending to assault the cult of muscularity that affected, in particular, the university men of the period. So he wanted to know how long young men trained for a boat race or for a running race. Would they come into contact with a 'low order' of professional instructor, thus leading to 'degrading social associations'? What kind of sporting slang would they use at a country-house party in the company of ladies and gentlemen? He disliked the cult of what was then known as 'muscular Christianity', with a passion for sports and a hopeless indifference to everything else. He was, in short, attacking the conventional English way of life and, as he put it, 'running full tilt against the popular sentiment'. He had decided to compose it first as a play, and had in fact completed the first act before changing his mind; since he was dealing with delicate material he would be more confident in writing a novel than a drama. He was not quite sure how a theatre audience might react.

A child born outside the bonds of matrimony can pose problems of its own. The first child of Martha Rudd and Wilkie Collins, to be known as Marian Dawson, was delivered by Frank Beard at Bolsover Street on 4 July 1869; the birth was not registered. Yet he had turned himself into William Dawson, barrister-at-law, for the sake of appearances. From this year he paid a regular monthly allowance of approximately £20 to 'Mrs Dawson', and also drew up a will for the first time. He had accepted all the appurtenances of married life without the ultimate declaration. This expressed the ambiguous status of Collins in the world, conventional and unconventional at the same time.

He had been concentrating on the new story to the exclusion of everything else, telling visitors and correspondents that he was 'out of town'. The birth of the baby interrupted his regimen of composition and preparation, perhaps, since in the autumn of 1869 he took refuge with the Lehmanns at The Woodlands in Highgate. They used to creep past his room, when he was at work. One of the children there, Rudolf Lehmann, remembered him as 'a neat figure of cheerful plumpness . . . not by any means the sort of man imagination would have pictured as the creator of Count Fosco and the inventor of the terrors of *Armadale* and the absorbing mystery of *The Moonstone*'.

He was a light and easy conversationalist. He told the Lehmann children stories of the famous prizefighter, Tom Sayers, whom Collins had often met. In fact Collins uses boxing metaphors in his correspondence which suggests that he had some interest in the sport. 'He hadn't any muscle to speak of in his forearm,' he told them, 'and there wasn't any show of biceps; but when I remarked on that, he asked me to observe his triceps and the muscle under his shoulder, and then I understood how he did it.' He also used to assist them with their homework.

The children also noticed that at Highgate Collins was 'a very hard and determined worker', a description eloquently amplified by his remark that 'I am nearly fagged to death'. He went off to Antwerp with Frank Beard for a period of recuperation; he just needed the voyage itself to revive him. Before he left he informed the Lehmanns that he had dedicated *Man and Wife* to them; he declared himself to be 'utterly worn out'. 'I am so weak,' he said, 'I can hardly write a note.' At the beginning of 1870 the 'gout in the eye' had returned, and for a while left him blind and helpless in a darkened room. His letters were in this period dictated to Carrie Graves. But he had recovered by the end of February.

On the day he completed the novel, 9 June, he fell asleep from sheer exhaustion. He was woken to be told that Charles Dickens was dead. He was 'shocked and grieved' at the news, but he must have sensed that his old friend was running perilously close to collapse. They were not in fact seeing each other as often as they had in the past. Collins may also have been hurt by the fact that Dickens had conceived a dislike for his brother; Dickens regarded his son-in-law as a burden and as a perpetual invalid. His energetic and vigorous nature could never have been very sympathetic to one who was perpetually ailing. Fechter noticed his glances at Charles Collins at the dinner table which might be interpreted as 'astonishing you should be here today; but tomorrow you will be in your chamber never to come out again'.

Collins said that the day of Dickens's funeral had been a 'lost day' in the sense that he had not been able to do any work. It does not suggest any deep or enduring grief. He met the train carrying Dickens's body at Charing Cross Station; he then travelled down Whitehall to Westminster Abbey in the last of the three carriages that followed the hearse. He shared the vehicle with his brother and with Frank Beard. The great years of promise and confidence had come to an end.

15

Bags of Blood

In the early summer of 1870 *Man and Wife* was published by the firm of F. S. Ellis in three volumes. Ellis was not an experienced publisher, and Collins believed that he was damaging the chances of the book by not advertising it properly. He was also concerned that the outbreak of the Franco-Prussian War in that summer would damage sales. He was worried unduly. The novel had run in *Cassell's Magazine* from the beginning of 1870 to the autumn, increasing the sales of that periodical to more than 70,000. The volume edition itself proved popular, largely because of its reference to pressing issues of the day, and two further editions were published that year.

The usual detailed and convoluted plot, in which Collins specialised, had a convincingly dramatic opening. The heroine of the novel, Anne Silvester, has been compromised by a famous athlete, Geoffrey Delmayn. But Delmayn wants to avoid the complications of marriage and persuades a friend, Arnold Brinkworth, to visit her in a Scottish inn where before witnesses they might be recognised as man and wife according to Scottish law. Arnold, unaware of the problem, then marries his own sweetheart. Just as Geoffrey is about to have Arnold's marriage annulled, so that he can be forced to take Anne as his wife, a letter is found from Geoffrey with a pledge to marry her. This is the clinching fact in obliging him to marry Anne, who now becomes the object of his murderous hatred.

The villain of the narrative is of course an exponent of muscular sportsmanship, and thus gives Collins the opportunity to attack those who prefer their biceps to their brains. 'We are readier than we ever were,' one character explains, 'to practise all that is rough in our national customs, and to excuse all that is violent and brutish in our national acts.' In this respect, as in others, he is concerned to break down the conventions of Victorian male society. It is of a piece, in this novel, with the marriage laws that overwhelmingly favour the male over the female.

The English reviewers were quick to castigate Collins for his less than enthusiastic portrait of the English sportsman. But the French critic, Louis Dépret, wrote that 'I have never seen in any other book the true youth of England so courageously presented'. A German reviewer said that 'it exactly describes the great multitude of Englishmen who discredit England with their coarse, shameless manners'. The enemies on the field could unite in their detestation of those English 'gentlemen' whom Collins also mocked.

Collins had been writing a dramatised version of *Man and Wife* at the same time as he continued with its serial publication, and the novel itself can certainly be conceived as a sequence of scenes. He relied upon dialogue and upon the sudden denouement, but it became clear enough in the course of his career that he was not an original dramatist; all his successful plays were adaptations of his novels.

He took what had now become his usual holiday after the publication of a novel, and on this occasion went on a cruise off the east coast. He also went to Lowestoft, and spent more time with the Lehmanns at Highgate. He wanted at all costs to avoid anything approaching literary work, and even locked up the paper he used for composition. In the autumn he travelled to Ramsgate; he had come to the seaside town as a child, with his family, and more recently with Caroline Graves. It is not clear whether on this occasion he was accompanied by Martha Rudd and their young daughter, but it seems very likely. In his next novel he described the diversions of the town, with its 'monkeys, organs, girls on stilts, a conjuror and a troop of negro minstrels'. In a subsequent novel, partly set in Ramsgate, he conjured up 'the cries of children at play, the shouts of donkey boys driving their poor beasts, the distant notes of brass instruments playing a waltz, and the mellow music of the small waves breaking on the sand'. Ramsgate had entered his imagination. He could wander to the harbour and hire a boat, or he could walk among the crowd of holidaymakers and admire with them the glittering sea.

Yet he was not one to rest for very long. He told a friend, in the winter of the year, that he wished 'to hit on some new method of appealing to the reader'. He was, for example, interested in the notion of writing shorter novels. This would save some of the expenses of production and at the same time lighten the task of the overtaxed reader. At the beginning of 1871 fresh intimations of a story came to him. It was a most unlikely one, concerning the love affair between a blind girl and a young man who has turned blue after drinking silver nitrate as a cure for epilepsy. Yet one definition of his art might be the pursuit of a plot through difficulties. He took out his papers and set to work.

Certain domestic events, however, must have to an extent marred his concentration. By the spring of 1871, at the latest, Caroline Graves had left her husband and returned to Gloucester Place after an absence of almost two years. She had become estranged from Joseph Clow for reason or reasons unknown, but of course she may also have missed the company of Collins and that of her daughter. In the census of 1871 she is described as 'widow' and as 'houskeeper and domestic servant'. She lived with him for the rest of his life, and took on the role of his companion. She and her daughter were often seen in public with him, attending the theatre or visiting the exhibitions. The two women also travelled abroad with him. One acquaintance, meeting him with the Lehmanns soon after Caroline's return, reported that he seemed in much better health and spirits, 'very bright and pleasant'.

Martha Rudd remained indistinctly in the background, although this spring she gave birth to another daughter, named as Harriet Dawson. Even if Martha Rudd never visited Gloucester Place, her children were always welcome there. Collins's family, morganatic or otherwise, was growing. To have two mistresses was, even by the standards of the nineteenth century, a precarious situation; but Collins seems to have adapted to it quite naturally and cheerfully. In his fiction he explored interesting or difficult relationships; in his life he remained inscrutable and imperturbable. In a letter to his solicitor concerning his will he refers to 'C' and to 'M', but that is one of the few references to Martha in his correspondence. There are, however, many allusions to 'the ladies' at Gloucester Place and to 'the two Carolines'. It is not at all clear that Martha Rudd resented her status; she may have accepted her role, grateful that she had been afforded security. Collins was always careful to make provision for her and her children, and no doubt his native kindliness and affability marked his relationship with the much younger woman.

In the autumn of 1871 his new novel, *Poor Miss Finch*, began its life in *Cassell's Magazine*. It was shorter than its predecessors, as he had planned, and lasted for six months before its publication in volume form by George Bentley. The firm of Bentley had introduced the work of Collins to the public more than twenty years before, and George Bentley now resumed the connection by offering £750 for the right to publish the serial.

In the same period *The Woman in White* finally reached the stage. A pirated version had been performed ten years before, at the time of the original publication, but this was Collins's version. It was a demanding production with interminable rehearsals lasting all day and sometimes half the night. Since the actor playing the role of Count Fosco was also the director, there was room for disagreements among the members of the cast. 'I marvelled at him,' one of the actors recorded, 'for authors as a rule are . . . the reverse of patient when attending the rehearsals of a piece they have written.' Collins, however, remained 'gentlemanly, patient and good-tempered, always ready with a smile if a chance offered itself or a peaceful word kindly suggesting when a point was to be gained'.

When it eventually opened at the Olympic on 9 October 1871, it lasted for four hours. Nevertheless it was a great success. The critic of *The Times* noted that Collins had 'firmly grasped the rarely appreciated truth, that situations which appear dramatic to a reader, are not necessarily dramatic when brought to the ordeal of the footlights'. Collins knew well enough that the popularity of the novel meant that its secrets had already been revealed. He dropped the meeting on Hampstead Heath; he developed scenes that he had only briefly employed in the novel, and generally relied more upon character than upon mystery. The audience loved it. Collins had remained in the dressing room in a state of nervous terror, but he was called forward at the end amid scenes of universal enthusiasm. It seemed that 'all London', or at least that part of it devoted to literary and artistic pursuits, was there. The run at the Olympic Theatre lasted for six months; extra chairs were put in the aisles, and prospective customers were turned away at the door. It was all, as Collins said, an 'immense success'. He had at last achieved his ambition of making money from the theatre.

The brief efflorescence of health did not last. In the early summer an attack of rheumatic gout confined him to his bed; once more the affliction went to his eyes and left him almost blind. One friend said that they 'were literally *enormous bags of blood*'. 'Do you know what colour her eyes are?' a character asks in a subsequent novel, *I Say No*. 'Red, poor soul – red as a boiled lobster.' He took 'electric baths' and went for drives in the fresh air; in the summer he tried the fine air of Upper Norwood, and was taking quinine as well as laudanum. But these were not proper remedies. There never was a time, in fact, when he was not recovering from a bout of illness or preparing for another. He had the appearance of a prematurely old man, and knew that he had before him the life of a semi-invalid more and more dependent upon opium.

Since he had already spent many days with a bandage around his eyes he naturally had some sympathy with the blind Miss Finch in the novel published at the beginning of 1872. It was subtitled 'A Domestic Story', and for some it was a little too domestic; one reviewer described it as 'a sensation novel for Sunday reading'. The plot itself is, in the abstract, ridiculous. A blind girl falls in love with a young man who is an identical twin; unfortunately his skin is discoloured by the treatment of silver nitrate for his epilepsy. A German eye surgeon restores Miss Finch's sight, whereupon the young man's identical brother – whose skin is perfectly pale – steps into his place. The consequent confusions are better perused than described. And of course all ends happily, the normal condition at the end of Collins's fictions.

Yet it has a strange power, also characteristic of Collins's novels. It is the power of curiosity, as the reader goes forward eagerly precisely to find out *what happens next*. Collins is very meticulous and methodical, leaving clues and evidences in the right places and invoking at all times 'coming events' or 'the light of later events' that will change the lives of the protagonists for ever. He hints perpetually at something 'under the surface', a 'hidden motive' or a 'terrible secret', that further provokes an insatiable curiosity. The reader is in a state of perpetual anticipation; as soon as one crisis is resolved, the author prepares another one. It is equivalent to a long walk in a landscape advertised by road signs and fingerposts; you simply have to go on.

Poor Miss Finch was not an overwhelming success and Bentley lost money on the venture. The story of the blind girl and the blue man was not to the public taste. It is sometimes said, in fact, that *Poor Miss Finch* marks the beginning of Collins's decline as an artist. He became a 'message' novelist, more concerned with polemic and argument than with style or invention. As Swinburne put it,

> What brought good Wilkie's genius nigh perdition?
> Some demon whispered – Wilkie! Have a mission!

This is snappy but it is not accurate. Collins never lost the habit – first evinced in *Ioláni* – of peppering his text with author-ial interjections; some were wise, some witty, some witty and wise, and some merely sententious. He did not sermonise as such, but the didactic element was always there. Collins did not have a 'mission', but he did have a *vision*, an understanding of human relations that he wished to propagate. The prefaces themselves advert to this. Yet he never allows any 'message' to override the imperatives of plot, while his dislike of such practices as vivisection lends power and purpose to his prose. He saw himself as an entertainer and a storyteller rather than a lecturer.

In truth his writing is all of a piece, from *Basil* to his final and uncompleted fiction. He had a genius for construction, above all else. He turned the process of telling a story into a formidable art. In his hands the sensation novel and the detective story became things of beauty precisely because he lends them an air of reality. Clarity of style, and lucidity of expression, were for him of para-mount importance. It is true that he had no genuine insight into the vagaries of human nature, but that is no reason to disqualify him as an artist. He was simply interested in other matters. His plots, for example, are perfectly calibrated mechanisms.

The Woman in White and *The Moonstone* may be the summit of his accomplishment, but novelists are often unjustly condemned for not being able to match their greatest achievements. All of his work remains powerful and ingenious, striking and persuasive. It is true that his later novels are no longer widely read, but modern taste is not impeccable. The themes and issues that haunted the Victorians may have been for a while exorcised; the conventions of the time that Collins attacked are now no longer pertinent. Yet he is still a living presence in English literature.

We may leave the last words on this matter to Count Fosco of *The Woman in White*. 'Habits of literary composition are perfectly familiar to me. One of the rarest of all the intellectual accomplishments that a man can possess is the grand faculty of arranging his ideas. Immense privilege! I possess it. Do you?'

16

Another Country

He had said, at the beginning of 1872, that he had no intention of beginning another long story for at least a year. He needed a rest. He wanted to get out of the country, but he first went back to Ramsgate in March. Two or three months later he made the familiar journey to Paris. His travelling companions for these two visits are not known, although the supposition must be that for at least one of them he was accompanied by Caroline and Carrie Graves. In the same period Martha Rudd herself moved to the Marylebone Road with her two young daughters; on a visit to a furniture store on the Tottenham Court Road, Hewetson & Thexton, she and Collins purchased a dining table, a sideboard, five dining chairs, a walnut bureau, a couch and an easy chair. She was not living in straitened circumstances. He was as usual unwell. 'Oh Christ,' he wrote to Lehmann in the summer, 'now the gout is gone, here comes the rheumatism.' His family were also in uproar; his three-year-old daughter, Marian Dawson, had broken her leg. Beard was summoned to mend it, which he did.

In the autumn of the year Collins was staying at Nelson Crescent, Ramsgate, for the first time. On this occasion he was with Caroline Graves. In this seaside town he set up a curious symmetry in his living arrangements. When he came down with Martha Rudd and the children he stayed at Wellington Crescent, immediately opposite Nelson Crescent on the other side of the bay. The households could therefore be respectably presented to two different landlords or landladies.

Yet even here he was still deeply at work, despite the unseasonably warm and muggy weather. He had not adhered to his resolution over the writing of a new novel. In the autumn of the year *The New Magdalen* appeared as a serial in *Temple Bar* magazine, a periodical edited by George Bentley that had superseded *Bentley's Miscellany*. It was expressly designed to be a drama as well as a novel and immediately begins on a sprightly note of theatrical invention.

Even as it was being serialised the highly respectable Charles Edward Mudie, founder of the largest of the circulating libraries, demanded a change in the title. 'Madgalen' was the name for a reformed prostitute. Collins of course refused, telling Bentley that 'nothing will induce me to modify the title . . . But the serious side of this affair is that this ignorant fanatic holds my circulation in his pious hands.' Collins may have deliberately chosen the story of a prostitute as a way of gaining sales; he might have wanted to bring back the public that had not appreciated *Poor Miss Finch*. In this strategy he appears to have been successful, since the sales of *Temple Bar* rose appreciably. He told Bentley that he was glad to hear that the first number had 'hit the mark' but that he was saving the strongest situations for later. By the spring of the year it was reported that *Temple Bar* had become 'the most sought after monthly of 1873'.

While the novel was being serialised *Man and Wife* opened at the Prince of Wales Theatre. After the success of *The Woman in White* Collins's expectations were high. It was, after all, an eminently dramatic story. It was staged by Squire and Marie Bancroft, two highly successful Victorian actors who had previously specialised in light comedy which became known as 'drawing-room comedy' or 'cup and saucer drama'. So *Man and Wife* was something of a departure for them. Once more Collins galvanised the theatrical world of London, and tickets were soon passing through the 'black market'. The *Daily Telegraph* noted that the audience on the opening night 'was almost wholly composed of those who have, in some form or other, won a social distinction of the most honourable kind'.

Collins was again beset with nervous terror, and spent the entire performance in Bancroft's dressing room. Yet his anxiety was misplaced. As he wrote to a friend 'it was certainly an extraordinary success. The pit got on its legs and cheered with all its might the moment I showed myself in front of the curtain.' The Bancrofts were known for the realism of their stage sets, which may have assisted the illusion, and for the first time on the London stage they used electric lighting for a storm scene. The theatre was always full. The Prince of Wales saw the play twice, on one occasion taking the tsarevich and tsarina of Russia. Collins had become the dramatist of the hour, and already the manager of the Olympic Theatre was trying to buy the rights of *The New Magdalen*.

Collins's elation, however, was quickly overtaken by events. At the beginning of April his brother, Charles Collins, died after a long period of illness. He seems finally to have succumbed to cancer of the stomach, but it is possible that he was consumptive. For all those around him the death was considered a release for him from unrelieved suffering. Collins reported that he had died 'without pain and without consciousness', but a friend reported that Collins was 'terribly broken down' after the event. He journeyed by train to Ramsgate in order to compose himself for a few days before the funeral.

Charles Collins's life had been an unhappy and perhaps unlucky one; he never achieved his older brother's success, and seems always to have been surrounded by people abler and more vigorous than himself. In his entry for the *Dictionary of National Biography*, Collins wrote that 'it was in the modest and sensitive nature of the man to underrate his own success. His ideal was a high one; and he never succeeded in satisfying his own aspirations.'

Collins told Bentley that 'I have hardly had a moment to

myself since the miserable day my brother died'. *The New Magdalen* was about to be published in volume form and he was already occupied with rehearsals for the stage version, to be played at the Olympic. He had to make sure that the drama was performed immediately after the book's release in order to avoid the danger of theatrical 'pirates' taking it over. One of the actors recalls him at the rehearsals sitting with his manuscript at a small table near the footlights making cuts and alterations as required.

The book was published on 17 May 1873, and the play opened two days later. *The New Magdalen* is the story of a reformed prostitute, Mercy Merrick, who steals the identity of a 'respectable' woman, Grace Roseberry, whom she has met on a battlefield of the Franco-Prussian War. She believes the lady to have been killed by a German shell, and therefore takes her clothes and papers so that she might begin a new life free of disgrace. She returns to England and, assuming the false identity, becomes the paid companion of a rich Englishwoman. Yet this is where the narrative springs to life. Grace Roseberry's life was saved by a surgeon. Now she appears in the house where Mercy is employed, determined to challenge the pretender to her name. Matthew Arnold stated that *The New Magdalen* was his favourite sensation novel, and it does have a raw dramatic power that excites and enthrals the reader; it conveys an extraordinary intensity and excitement.

He met one such reader in a railway car. A clergyman and his two daughters were travelling with him. When the clergymen fell asleep one of the young ladies quietly took out a book from her bag; she dropped it and, when Collins retrieved it for her he saw that it was *The New Magdalen*. She blushed as she realised that her secret reading was discovered. 'It's perfectly dreadful,' she told her sister. But soon enough she was thoroughly absorbed in it. On signs that her father was about to wake, she quickly returned the book to her bag. When Collins looked at her, she blushed again.

The stage version itself was an immense success, and Collins had to take an unprecedented curtain call between the acts as well as at the finale. He told George Bentley that 'I don't think I ever saw such enthusiasm in the theatre before'. It was revived many times throughout the nineteenth century, and silent film versions were screened before the First World War.

He had hoped that the success of the play would guarantee a large sale of the novel, and that the clamour of the public would force Mudie to buy large quantities for his circulating libraries. Yet there was no such demand, and a large number of unsold copies was left on Bentley's hands. Collins himself was so discouraged by this relative failure that he seriously considered giving up the trade of storytelling and concentrating upon the theatre instead.

Yet at the same time other employment offered itself. In the spring of the year he received a proposal for a reading tour of the United States. Other English novelists, most notably Charles Dickens, had proved that travelling from city to city with book in hand was a profitable enterprise. Collins himself speculated that he would make a large sum out of it, and he assented. He had, first of all, to prepare himself. At a charity matinee at the Olympic in the summer he read an expanded version of his short story, 'A Terribly Strange Bed'. He knew well enough that he could not cut up the intricate mechanism of his ingenious plots, and that he must rely instead on the tone and atmosphere of his shorter fiction.

The summer reading had a mixed response. Percy Fitzgerald, the journalist, reported that it was 'singularly tame . . . clever man as he was, the impression he produced was that of all things in the world he had selected the one for which he was the least fitted'. Frank Archer, the actor, said that 'he lacked the physique and varied gifts for a public reader, but what he did I thought was earnest and impressive'. A review in the *Pall Mall Gazette* warned him to take on the role of a lecturer rather than an actor;

'otherwise, he will expose himself to the ridicule of the unfeeling'. Short and prematurely aged, he did not have the commanding presence of a born performer. He would have to play to his strengths and, with that in mind, he prepared himself for the Atlantic voyage.

He sailed for America on 13 September, but before he left England, he arranged his affairs in good order. He drew up a new will in which he made ample provision for Martha Rudd and her children as well as for Caroline Graves and her daughter. He had also asked his solicitor, William Tindell, to take care of both families in his absence. He also insured Martha's new furniture. He boarded the *Algeria* at Liverpool and, after an unremarkable voyage, arrived in New York harbour twelve days later. Fechter was waiting to greet him on the quayside, and escorted Collins to the Westminster Hotel where they dined together. 'You will find friends here wherever you go,' Fechter told him.

There were friends, and reporters, in large numbers. He was aware of his popularity in America, which was second only to that of Dickens himself. The sales of *The New Magdalen*, for example, had been enormous in comparison with those of England. Since there was no copyright agreement with America, however, his rewards were not as high as they might have been. He was told that one American publisher had sold 120,000 copies of *The Woman in White*, to which Collins's response was that 'he never sent me sixpence'. Nevertheless his real American publishers, Harper & Brothers, issued a new 'Library Edition' in honour of his arrival. The newspapers carried accounts of his activities even before his first reading.

On 27 September, for example, he was guest of honour at the Lotos Club in the presence of many New York worthies; he delivered a speech in which he interpreted his welcome as 'a recognition of English literature, liberal, spontaneous and sincere'. In this first week on American soil he was living in what he called a 'social whirlwind' with dinners and breakfasts and meetings and speeches. A breakfast for twenty-four people at the Union Club in New York included strong drink, speeches and canvasback duck.

Like other famous English visitors he found the attentions of the press very disagreeable. They waited for him in corridors and in public rooms; they even followed him into private houses. One afternoon Collins had made a call upon an acquaintance when their meeting was interrupted by a lady with 'a little black dog in one hand and her card in the other'. She represented one of the newspapers and wanted a few minutes' conversation. Collins turned to his hostess, in order to apologise for the impertinence, but the hostess thought nothing of it. She laughed and said that it was the journalist's 'daily bread'. It was the difference between an American and an English sensibility.

He was so pestered by journalists, in fact, that he arranged to meet them in groups rather than individually. On one occasion he was confronted by a posse of twelve female journalists waiting for him in the sitting room of his hotel. 'Let me embrace you for the company,' one of them said. According to Collins she was 'the oldest and the ugliest . . . I suppose I did look grim, for I felt it'.

Yet he was generally beguiled and charmed by the Americans whom he met. They were frank, cheerful and free; they did not obey the conventions of Victorian England that Collins himself cordially detested. They lacked the hypocrisy and frigid good manners of the English middle class. They had minor failings, however; they did not hum or whistle; they did not keep dogs; and they never walked anywhere.

He had committed himself only to ten readings, and he gave the first of them in Albany. Here he read an expanded version of 'The Dream Woman', the story of the murderous wife. He asked his audience to imagine themselves to be a group of friends seated in a parlour with an old acquaintance; this was precisely the mood which Dickens tried to summon before his own readings. Collins went on to remind them that he was not an actor. He would not, in other words, emulate Dickens's manner. He told an English friend that 'my way of reading surprises them . . . because I don't flourish a paper knife and stamp about the platform, and thump the reading desk'. These were all aspects of Dickens's public readings. Collins was altogether a more modest and self-effacing figure. Yet he seemed to be a success. The first reading 'so arrested the audience that not a soul stirred'. He did have the power of story-telling if not of personality.

He read 'The Dream Woman' in Philadelphia also, in the middle of October, but one newspaper reviewer commented that 'it was not pleasant to hear a famous Englishman describing, before several hundred pure girls, how one wretched, fallen woman, after mysteriously killing her man, had captivated two more, and stabbed another to death in a drunken frenzy'. Collins's sensationalism was sometimes too strong for the sensitive.

He gave two or three readings in Boston at the end of the month, and the music hall in particular was 'crowded to every part'. The *Boston Evening Transcript* reported that 'he gave evidence of great power in facial expression and a good command over his voice'. One lady in high Bostonian society was not so impressed. Annie Fields complained that 'his talk was rapid and pleasant but not at all inspiring . . . A man who had been feted and petted in London society, who has overeaten and overdrunk, has been ill, is gouty, and in short is no very wonderful specimen of a human being.'

At the beginning of November he returned to New York in order to assist a production of *The New Magdalen* at the Broadway Theatre. This was almost as successful as its London counterpart, with calls of 'Collins, Collins' from the audience at the end of the fourth act; he came before the curtain three times to acknowledge the applause. The New York critics, however, were more easily shocked than their London colleagues by this story of a reformed prostitute. The reviewer for the *Daily Graphic* wrote that 'a play so utterly vicious, so shamefully profligate in its teaching, has never before been produced at a New York theatre'. Nevertheless it remained a favourite of the public and, after three weeks in the city, began an extended tour of the country.

On the evening after the first night's performance, Collins read 'The Dream Woman' from a desk on the stage of the Association Hall. The audience, according to the *New York Times*, 'hung in breathless silence on the reader's words' together with 'a large number of young ladies who watched the reader with that steadfast fixity of gaze which only ladies can fasten on a gentleman of literary eminence'. His fame preceded him everywhere. While walking in the streets of New York, on his way to another public breakfast, he was stopped by a young man who recognised him from his photographs. The young man asked for his autograph and promptly produced a piece of paper, a pen and an ink bottle from his pockets. 'How am I to write it?' Collins asked him.

'You can write it on my back.' He turned round and gave him 'a back' as if they were playing leapfrog. Collins was astounded.

Despite his fragile health Collins survived the long train journeys from city to city. He even managed to endure a journey of fifteen hours from Montreal to Toronto, albeit with the assistance of dry champagne and a cold turkey. Toronto left him feeling rheumatic, and the prospect of Niagara left him underwhelmed. 'What will the waterfall do? Besides I don't like waterfalls – they are noisy.' In the event, however, he was suitably impressed.

At the beginning of 1874 he returned to the United States with the intention of travelling west. He had originally hoped to reach Salt Lake City, the home of the Mormons, but got no further than Chicago. The incessant travelling by railway did now begin to affect his health, and he found it impossible to find rest in the sleeping cars. He was not sorry to leave Chicago where 'the dull sameness of the great blocks of iron and brick overwhelm me'. He decided to turn back to Boston, and over the next two months he read in various New England towns. The dry air of that region was of material benefit to him. He had not one ache or pain, and the gout left him entirely. 'In *your* country,' he told one American acquaintance, 'I felt five and twenty years old. In *my* country, I (not infrequently) feel five and ninety.'

At Boston a reception was given for Collins in which the great American authors – Longfellow and Twain among them – came to pay their respects. Mark Twain made a speech, and Oliver Wendell Holmes recited a poetic tribute. Each gentleman was then presented with a bon-bon box, covered in Turkey morocco, which contained the photograph and the autograph of the English author.

He had originally intended to stay in America until the end of March, but news from England hastened his departure. Martha Rudd's landlord wished to sell the house on the Marylebone Road, thereby obliging Martha and her two daughters to leave, unless 'Mr Dawson' would consent to buy the lease. Collins did not wish to do so and, although Martha had three months' notice, he now had to find his family somewhere else to live.

He had made approximately £2,500 from his extended reading tour; it was only a tenth of what Dickens had gathered, but it was enough to make the journey worthwhile. He had earned less because, for the sake of his health, he could not read more. Yet he had thoroughly enjoyed the experience; he had made new friends and had enjoyed the unaffected admiration of his audiences. 'The enthusiasm and kindness are really and truly beyond description', he wrote. 'I should be the most ungrateful man living if I had any other than the highest opinion of the American people.' On 7 March he took the *Parthia* from Boston to Liverpool.

17

Clap-Trap

He landed at Liverpool on 18 March and had returned to London by the following day. He made his way to Gloucester Place, but must have gone very soon afterwards to Martha Rudd and the two daughters in Marylebone Road. That reunion is not in doubt, since Martha gave birth to their third child nine months and seven days later.

The most urgent matter was to find her a new house but clearly Martha, or Collins's solicitor, had anticipated him. Only a week after his return the family had moved to Taunton Place, a few yards north of their previous address; it was one in a row of cottages close to Regent's Park where she and her growing family were to live for the next fifteen years. Such a cottage, 'in a by-road, just outside the park', is described in a subsequent novel. It was on two floors, with three rooms on each floor; it was 'simply and prettily furnished; and it was completely surrounded by its own tiny plot of garden-ground'. This was to be the principal site of Collins's family life. 'Work, walk, visit to my morganatic family,' he told Frederick Lehmann, 'such is life.' There were benefits, however; he believed that it was sometimes possible to 'walk off' his rheumatism. As soon as he returned, however, he became afflicted by all of his English ailments; his eyes turned yellow, and his head ached.

The fact that he now had the responsibility of a third child made him look to his finances. There was no respite from the continual labour of composition and soon after his return from the United States he began work on what was to become his thirteenth novel. *The Law and the Lady* began its serialisation, in the *Graphic*, in the autumn of this year. He also arranged for a 'novelisation' of *The Frozen Deep* in *Temple Bar* magazine and contributed a short story, 'A Fatal Fortune', to *All the Year Round* now under the management of Charles Dickens junior.

He was also concerned to 'work' his copyrights. He had been about to sign an agreement with George Bentley to reprint all of his old novels in a cheaper edition; he had told Bentley that he had been obliged to make some large payments 'and there are more "outgoings" looming on the horizon', no doubt in the shape of an infant. He was about to sign an arrangement when a relatively inexperienced publisher, Andrew Chatto, stepped forward with a better offer. He agreed to pay Collins the sum of £2,000 for the right to publish all of Collins's earlier fictions; he was to be given a seven-year licence, while Collins himself retained the copyrights. It was an advantageous offer and, in time, Collins's novels were issued in two-shilling editions; it was a move towards that larger public of which he had written. All of Collins's subsequent novels were published under the imprint of Chatto & Windus.

Collins's third child, and first son, was born on Christmas Day 1874. Collins informed his solicitor that he had been presented with 'a Christmas box in the shape of a big boy'. He named him William Charles Dawson in recognition of his father and brother; in accordance with a new law the birth was registered by Martha Rudd two months later. The child soon became known as 'little Charley'. Another Christmas memento may be mentioned here. Collins had Christmas greetings printed on small cards, with some of his novels named beside his photograph. 'Wishing you a Happy Christmas. *Hide and Seek* 'neath the mistletoe, played for a kiss – I hope you may try it tonight – I mention *No Name*, *A Dead Secret* is this, with some beautiful *Woman in White*.'

The Law and the Lady was published by Chatto in February

1875, at first in the familiar three-volume format so vital to the interests of the circulating libraries. It was in essence a murder mystery without a murder, revolving around the Scottish verdict of 'not proven'. Valeria Macallan has married a man who is immensely secretive about his past; it transpires that Eustace has married her under a false name, not wanting her to know that he had been tried for the murder of his first wife only to be acquitted on the verdict of 'not proven' rather than 'not guilty'. Valeria sets out to prove his innocence, thus joining the company of Collins's female detectives.

It is all very ingenious and very entertaining, with the complex marital relations of Eustace Macallan acting as a lightning rod for Collins's own peculiar situation. 'Don't ask!' he tells his bride. 'Don't look!' He is much older than she, has a beard streaked with grey and walks with a limp. It is by no means a self-portrait, but it bears a passing resemblance to the novelist himself. A legless invalid also enters the plot as a nightmare image of Collins; Miserrimus Dexter is cared for by a simple-minded cousin to whom he relates long stories. 'Her great delight is to hear me tell a story. I puzzle her to the verge of distraction; and the more I confuse her the better she likes the story.' He has a powerful imaginative life, but it is one marked by cruelty and lust. Again it is not a self-portrait but the novel allows the author to fantasise about certain tendencies within his own character. On one occasion Dexter dresses in pink silk; Collins wore pink shirts.

It was not to the taste of the critics who suggested that it was, in the words of the *Athenaeum*, 'an outrageous burlesque upon himself'. There are indeed elements of the circus about it as Collins parades some of his pet obsessions. The reviewer of the *Leader* remarked that to him 'life is in the most literal sense a riddle and an enigma. The causes of human actions must be sought in dark corners and in crooked ways . . . He dwells in a world of strange and lurid imaginings, which is entirely his own.' But if *The Law and the Lady* is touched by phantasmagorical desires, it is also a well-disciplined and well-executed mystery story with an ending that will come as a surprise to most readers. In sum it represents all the driven, wilful, energetic aspects of mid-Victorian civilisation. The public was also kinder than the critics; Collins held on to his readership, and there is no sign of any decline in sales.

He had gone on his travels once again, as was his custom at the end of any long project. He visited Paris for a week and then, to preserve his failing health, had made his way to the eastern coast. He was having trouble with his kidneys. In October he determined to try Brussels and Antwerp, in the company of Caroline Graves, in order to prepare himself for the ordeal of the coming winter. No sooner had he returned, however, than he set to work on another novel 'with a touch of the supernatural in it'. *The Two Destinies* has the unfortunate distinction of being the least successful of Collins's novels, although on this occasion a more than usually painful period of 'gout in the eye' may act as an excuse for some of its weaknesses; he was forced to dictate passages to Carrie Graves, and the monthly parts were shorter than usual. He was in any case living like a hermit, going nowhere and seeing nobody.

The Two Destinies narrates the strange fate of two lovers who are separated early in their romantic lives; they meet again unexpectedly but, for reasons that remain partially obscure, they are unable to recognise each other. There follows a number of supernatural visitations where the two lovers call to one another, in dream or apparition; after a number of melodramatic adventures, they are finally reunited when she recognises a childhood memento which he has carried with him everywhere. It is the merest hokum made up of sentiment and sentimentality; yet it is also evidence of how much his touch might falter under the burden of severe ill health.

Curiously for Collins, also, it incorporates all the most obvious

Victorian conventions in which the merest allusion to sexuality would break the spell of over-anxious and over-refined men and women. In an age when some women were traded on the streets it was all the more important for a gentlewoman to be completely pure and completely untouched. If a man put his hand upon her arm, she called out for help. This is the atmosphere of *The Two Destinies*. When Collins's critical faculties are in abeyance he falls back upon Victorian sentiment; when his intellect is clouded, he reverts to the standards of conventional morality.

Yet his dramatic activities showed no sign of abating. An adaptation of *Armadale*, *Miss Gwilt*, opened in Liverpool before 'going in' to the capital. 'We had great luck,' Collins said of the performance at the Alexandra Theatre in Liverpool. 'The audience received the piece with open arms.' He was not so sanguine about the London production at the Globe Theatre in Newcastle Street. The scenery was not completed and the management of the theatre was in the hands of 'incapable idiots and blackguards'; when he visited the theatre one evening, at eight o'clock, the carpenters were all drunk. Such was his dismay that he was afraid to ask any of his acquaintance to the first night. He predicted a disaster but, to his delight, the public were entertained and amused by the production.

Miss Gwilt was essentially a new work, having been extensively rewritten to protect the sensibilities of the English public who might not relish the portrayal of an unapologetic bigamist and murderer on the stage. She becomes a more sympathetic figure, more sinned against than sinning.

Eight months later, in November 1876, a production of *No Thoroughfare* opened at the Olympic Theatre in Wych Street; the manager, however, had incurred Collins's displeasure by choosing a cast without his approval. He declined to have anything more to do with the production, other than the stipulation that it should have a guaranteed run of thirty nights. Yet he relented, and eventually agreed to attend the rehearsals. In the following summer *The Dead Secret* opened at the Lyceum, and in the early autumn it was succeeded by a production of *The Moonstone* at the Royal Olympic. The latter was not a success. Collins had 'adapted' it almost out of existence, with the removal of several key characters and the excision of any reference to opium. It lasted for nine weeks only.

He had been in the habit of taking short vacations, to Paris and Switzerland and elsewhere, as a way of 'laying in' a stock of good health; when his brain was 'fagged' with overwork or when he had survived a more than usually uncomfortable bout of rheumatic gout, he longed to remove himself to the dry air of the Continent. In the summer of 1877 he was so crippled that he could enter a carriage only with difficulty. It was time to escape the unwholesome atmosphere of London. So in the autumn of the year he proposed a more adventurous tour of the Tyrol and of northern Italy with Caroline Graves; Carrie Graves remained in London to deal with the management of the household as well as correspondence in which she referred to Collins as her 'godfather' or 'godpapa'. The position of Caroline Graves was now settled beyond the possibility of any doubt. She was his official companion.

He decided to travel wherever the prospect of dry air took him. He and Caroline rested at Brussels, and then proceeded in slow stages to Munich. They travelled erratically in northern Italy, and reached Venice by the end of November; the fruit of the sojourn in Venice was a frantic piece of Grand Guignol, 'The Haunted Hotel', that was eventually serialised in *Belgravia* magazine. It had been a serpentine journey in search of health which seems to have succeeded; he reported a great improvement in morale and strength to support him in the face of the coming winter. His friends told him that he looked twenty years younger. But it was his last trip to the Continent.

His domestic arrangements were about to change when in the spring of the following year Carrie Graves married a respectable young solicitor to whose practice Collins transferred his business. On her marriage certificate, registering her union with Mr Henry Bartley, she followed her mother's practice by reducing her age by three years; she also described her father as 'captain in the army' when he had in fact been a solicitor's clerk. Three daughters appeared in quick succession. Collins became godfather to the first of them, but all were embraced within the larger family.

Carrie still acted as Collins's amanuensis whenever possible, but there were times when other secretarial help was needed. His working habits, however, were now fixed. By the window of his study on the first floor of Gloucester Place stood a large writing table, fitted with a shabby desk; he had retained this portable desk since his schooldays. Beside it was a box containing notes for stories and for characters. Here also were two books of cuttings from the newspapers, one entitled 'hints for scenes and incidents' and the other entitled 'hints for character'.

He revised endlessly, with many alterations and substitutions and crossings-out making a mess of his manuscripts. He always used a quill pen. The manuscripts gave the impression that he was, as Walter de la Mare put it, 'lapped in the condition of the worm in the cocoon spun out of its own entrails; ink his nectar, solitude his paradise, the most exhausting earthly work at once his joy, his despair, his anodyne and his incentive'. The first revision was given to the copyist, and then the copyist's manuscript was subject to two more revisions before being sent to the printer. The printer's proof was then revised, and sent back for correction. When it passed from periodical to volume form, it was corrected once more. He also owned a 'Hektograph', a machine that could make multiple copies from an original. He was always a hard worker, even though he tended to complain of the consequent fatigue.

Certainly there was no diminution of effort and concentration in his later years. At the beginning of 1879 a new novel began its serialisation in the *World*. *The Fallen Leaves* is devoted to the outcasts of the Victorian world. It is in part concerned with the reclamation of a prostitute by a young Christian socialist with the inauspicious name of Amelius Goldenheart. He warned his Canadian publisher that 'I am treating some very difficult and delicate subjects this time'. He derived his young American hero from Charles Nordhoff's *The Communistic Societies of the United States* and in particular from the account of the Oneida communities in New York and in New England; he pitted the young man's socialism against the tyrannical forces of the contemporary world. 'On the floor of a kitchen, men, women and children lay all huddled together in closely packed rows. Ghastly faces rose terrified out of the seething obscurity, when the light of the lantern fell on them. The stench drove Amelius back, sickened and shuddering.' When Goldenheart marries the prostitute it might seem that the forces of goodwill win through, but any lasting resolution is still in doubt.

It was a success neither with the critics nor with the public. It was considered 'low'. He had been planning a sequel but the poor sales deterred him from trying the experiment; in his next book he said that *The Fallen Leaves* had reached 'only a comparatively limited class of reader in England'. He had hoped that a six-shilling edition would sell, but he was to be disappointed. The subject was, perhaps, just a little too risqué even for the more enlightened Victorian reader.

It is in fact one of his most ambitious and polemical novels in which he assaults what he described as 'the clap-trap morality' of his contemporaries. Throughout all of his work he strives to undermine what might be called the masculine structures of society – whether it be in the sexual ambiguity of his characters, in his ridicule of the cult of muscularity, or in his direct onslaught on the property rights of husbands. 'The world is hard on women,' one of the characters in *The Fallen Leaves* reflects, 'and the rights of property is a damned bad reason for it.' Victorian business is denounced as an 'imposture' and a 'masquerade', with the unspoken assumption that other aspects of nineteenth-century society are involved in the same illusion. In a phrase from the novel, 'the men have settled it so'. In the middle of the century a term had come to epitomise this state of bondage; it became known as 'the system'.

In defiance of these man-made constraints Collins took for his heroines independent and strong-minded women who rise above their conventional roles. He reserves his contempt for the males who, as in *Man and Wife*, are 'all profoundly versed in horse-racing, in athletic sports, in pipes, beer, billiards and betting. All profoundly ignorant of everything else under the sun.'

The religion of the nineteenth century also comes under attack in *The Fallen Leaves*. 'The Christian religion, as Christ taught it,' another character declares, 'has long ceased to be the religion of the Christian world. A selfish and cruel Pretence is set up in its place.' Goldenheart says, of the House of Lords, that 'that assembly is not elected by the people, and it therefore has no right to existence in a really free country'. As for the House of Commons, 'modern members belong to classes of the community which have really no interest in providing for popular needs and lightening popular burdens'. They also were frauds. It is a common mistake, of course, to confuse character with author; but it is hard not to suspect some authorial sympathy with Goldenheart's sentiments. *The Fallen Leaves* is one of the most powerful and impassioned critiques of Victorian society ever composed by a novelist. He dedicated the novel 'to CAROLINE'.

18

Breast Pangs

Ramsgate had now become his chosen resort, a sure resting place and refuge. He hated Brighton, where for some reason he could neither eat nor sleep; the town brought him out in 'cold perspiration'. He avoided Broadstairs, also, because it contained too many memories of happier days with Dickens and his family; it had become for him 'the most dreadful place in the world'. So it was Ramsgate. The sea air acted on him as a restorative, and his doctor recommended frequent applications of it. He told Edward Pigott that 'Beard seems to think that my destiny is to *live* at Ramsgate'. With two establishments to maintain in London, that was impracticable. Nevertheless he arranged to spend more and more time on the sea coast.

He could reach it by steamer or by train from London Bridge Station. He hired a steam-yacht, the *Phyllis*, that was moored in the harbour; he described it as 'a lovely little steam-launch . . . the admiration of nautical mankind. The engineer is bigger than the funnel, and can only just squeeze himself into the engine-room.' He used to say that the perfection of enjoyment could only be found 'when you are at sea in a luxurious well-appointed steam-yacht in lovely summer weather'.

He would stay with Caroline at 14 Nelson Crescent, or with Martha at 27 Wellington Crescent where he was known as William Dawson. The families – now including Carrie's daughters as well as Martha's children – mingled happily together; Martha and Caroline, however, never met. He would write at his portable desk in the morning and then spend the time in fishing, walking, or sailing; he would be at sea for two or three hours at a stretch.

Yet work was never very far from his mind. 'Surely,' a character remarks to himself in a subsequent novel, *Heart and Science*, 'I may finish a chapter, before I go to sea tomorrow?' Only two months after the publication of *The Fallen Leaves*, a new novel started with a newspaper syndication. *Jezebel's Daughter* appeared as a serial in the *Bolton Weekly Journal* and twelve other newspapers of northern England; the arrangement was made with an entrepreneur, William Frederic Tillotson, who had set up a 'Fiction Bureau' to market novels in as wide a fashion as possible. Collins, always eager to reach and to exploit a new audience, readily concurred.

At the beginning of 1880 he reported to Andrew Chatto that he had a 'new story ready for book publication'. He expressed some hesitation that he might be going ahead a little too fast for his publisher; he was aware of the perils of overproduction. In the event *Jezebel's Daughter* sold well.

The novel was in effect a reworking, or rewriting, of *The Red Vial*; this was the melodrama that had been performed more than twenty years before, and had effectively been laughed off the stage. Collins clearly hoped that time would be once more a great healer with the reprise of an idiot, a female poisoner, and a rising from the dead in a mortuary. Once more he invokes the power of destiny in the life of his characters. 'Never could any poor human creature have been a more innocent instrument of mischief in the hands of Destiny than I was, on that fatal journey.' Once more he relies upon the machinery of outrageous coincidence. And once more he introduces letters and other documents to lend authenticity to the narrative. But these are the pleasures, not the problems, of the plot. It takes an exquisite art to bring matters to fulfilment at a gradual and steady pace, to baffle expectations, to add ingenious clues and contrivances. It requires much caution and concentration. That is why Collins was exhausted at the end of each novel.

His appearance might have given some cause for concern. Julian Hawthorne, the son of the novelist, was a visitor to Gloucester Place during this period. He described him as 'soft, plump, and pale, suffered from various ailments, his liver was wrong, his heart weak, his lungs faint, his stomach incompetent . . . his air was of mild discomfort'. He also had acquired 'a queer way of holding his hand, which was small, plump and unclean, hanging up by the wrist, like a rabbit on its hind legs . . . One felt that he was unfortunate and needed succour.' Hall Caine, a young novelist, recalled that he had a 'vague and dreamy look sometimes seen in the eyes of the blind, or those of a man to whom chloroform has just been administered'.

Edmund Yates, a friend of early date, described him as 'very bent and gnarled and gnome-like, very much changed, indeed, from the dapper little man I had met thirty years before'. Frank Beard's son completes the portrait with the image of him 'walking up the street with the aid of a heavy stick, bowed nearly doubled, and looking like an old man of eighty, though he was but sixty-five'.

Collins believed that Tillotson's syndication of *Jezebel's Daughter* had been a success; and so, in the autumn of 1880, his new novel appeared in the *Sheffield and Rotherham Independent Supplement* as well as in other provincial newspapers. *The Black Robe* is an account of a Jesuit priest, Father Benwell, who wishes by any available means to obtain the estate of an English gentleman for his order. He believes it to have been improperly stolen from its rightful owners by Henry VIII, and plots to have it bequeathed to the Church by its present possessor. It is an ingenious and entertaining story that appealed to a contemporary audience whose anti-Catholic prejudices were already well known. Nevertheless Collins told an acquaintance that the novel was considered 'in

Roman Catholic countries as well as Protestant England to be the best thing I have written for some time'.

He was not aware of any diminution in the quality or the value of his writing, and in this period he approached a representative of the new profession of literary agent in order to protect his interests. Alexander Pollock Watt had set up his agency a few years previously, and had already acquired a high reputation. Since Collins now had approximately twenty novels in print, with all the attention to contracts and payments they required, it was natural for him to seek professional assistance. It could save him time as well as make him money. He had grown tired of dealing personally with the managers of the provincial newspapers, for example, whom he called 'curious savages'.

So at the beginning of December 1881, he consulted Watt on the next novel that he planned for newspaper syndication. He was already plotting a new play by the time he had completed *The Black Robe*, but an idea for a new novel would not let him rest. *Heart and Science* was a powerful statement of his belief in the dehumanising effect of science in general and of the practice of vivisection in particular. His audience now included the 'unknown public' he had once assiduously courted; one of the newspapers that printed the instalments of the novel was the *South London Press*. By June he had sent the first six chapters to Chatto, for publication in Chatto's *Belgravia* magazine, with the message that 'my own vainglorious idea is that I have never written such a first number since *The Woman in White*'. He became so wildly excited by the story that he wrote day after day, without any rest; on one day he worked for twelve hours at a stretch. He wrote furiously for six months, when he was 'one part sane and three parts mad', but during that period he never once suffered from gout. He contemplated the end of the narrative with growing excitement that left him exhausted. As soon as he had completed the novel, the affliction came back.

Heart and Science is one of Collins's most unjustly neglected novels. It contains some of his most vividly imagined characters, as if his simple distaste could bring people to life. Mrs Gallilee is a woman of scientific interests. 'I have always maintained that the albuminoid substance of frogs' eggs is insufficient (viewed as nourishment) to transform a tadpole into a frog – at last, the professor owns that I am right. I beg your pardon, Carmina; I am carried away by a subject that I have been working at in my stolen intervals for weeks past.'

Dr Benjulia, the vivisectionist, is also one of his most comic creations. He had a propensity for tickling a little girl named Zo with the cap at the end of his cane. 'I wish I could tickle her some more,' he says before meeting his death. Does the vivisectionist love Zo, or does he think of her as another specimen? There are subtleties of characterisation in this novel that are generally believed to be beyond Collins's reach.

The small girl herself is a convincing creation. Here is her description of a Scotsman. 'He skirls on the pipes – skirls mean screeches. When you first hear him, he'll make your stomach ache. You'll get used to that – and you'll find you'll like him. He wears a purse and a petticoat; he never had a pair of trousers on in his life; there's no pride about him. Say you're my friend and he'll let you smack his legs.' Of her cousins she remarks, 'Nice girls – they play at everything I tell 'em. Jolly boys – when they knock a girl down, they pick her up again, and clean her.' Her speech is a token of the vivacious and boisterous tone of the entire narrative.

The reviewers, sensing a return to Collins's old form, were enthusiastic. The *Academy* reported that it was 'thoroughly readable and enthralling from its first page to its last'. One critic remarked that if *The Woman in White* was 'written in blood and vitriol', *Heart and Science* was written with 'blood and dynamite'. His most ferocious attack was upon vivisection itself, a practice much discussed and debated at the time; Collins, with his strong attachment to animals, violently disapproved. 'My last experiments on a monkey horrified me,' Benjulia says. 'His cries of suffering, his gestures of entreaty, were like those of a child.' He opts to continue his experiment. Collins suggests, rather than describes, the horrors. This renders them all the more fearful. According to Collins himself, 'the literary critics congratulate me on the production of a masterpiece'.

The relative success was followed by a relative disaster. Ever since completing *The Black Robe* he had been working on a new play. *Rank and Riches* opened at the Adelphi Theatre in the early summer of 1883. It had a strong cast, including George Alexander and Charles Hawtrey, but not even the most prestigious casting could save it. The plot itself was complicated, including a 'bird doctor', a consumptive employee of a communist club, and the startling revelation that certain peers of the realm were the illegitimate children of a bigamous marriage. It can be construed as another assault by Collins on the conventions of Victorian social life.

At the preliminary readings the theatrical producers had predicted another triumph for the author, and he appeared at the first night with a large camellia in his buttonhole. He may perhaps have already been rehearsing his speech at the curtain calls. It did not quite go to plan. When the 'bird doctor' appeared on stage, scattering birdseed in all directions, the audience began to howl. Sir Arthur Wing Pinero, then a young English actor and dramatist, recalled the occasion. 'Everything went wrong. The audience, amused by some awkwardly phrased expressions, tittered; then, as the play advanced, broke into unrestrained laughter; and finally, enraged by an indignant protest from one of the actors, hooted the thing unmercifully.' The protest had come from George Anson who at the interval had advanced in front of the footlights and denounced the audience as 'a lot of damned cads' who had insulted a 'great master'. There were shouts of 'Bosh!', 'Nonsense!' and

'Get on with the play!' One of the actresses, Alice Lingard, had already broken down in tears.

Rank and Riches, now known as Rant and Rubbish, had failed. The dramatic critic of *The Times* said that 'the want of dramatic purpose in the play – as a result of which the characters seemed to flounder aimlessly about – combined with action bordering at times upon burlesque, and a prevalence of unlucky lines, was more than the public could be expected to endure'.

Collins withdrew the play after a week's run. He declared that the audience had not understood the drama; they had not sympathised with the characters, either, who introduced a perfectly new element onto the English stage. He was, naturally enough, aggrieved. He and his actors had been 'brutally treated'; even the women had been personally insulted. The 'jeering and hooting' during the second act were succeeded by 'yells of laughter' in the third. He added only that strangers offered him their sympathy and indignation. Yet he was not entirely cast down. He was ready to give it a 'new trial' elsewhere.

He was further reassured by the success, a few months later, of *The New Magdalen* at the Novelty Theatre in Great Queen Street. He did not attend the first night on this occasion; whether he was absent as a result of neuralgia, as he said, or of nerves, is unknown. After the failure at the Adelphi, however, he never wrote another play for the London theatre.

Yet he was still sustained by the success of *Heart and Science*, and almost immediately set to work upon another serialisation. He wanted to beat the American pirates, and so promised Harper & Brothers that he would present them with a complete manuscript three months before the end of its serialisation in England. There would then be no possibility of the pirates anticipating them. This of course meant unflagging composition, against the advice of Frank Beard, and the last ten chapters of the novel were written without any intermission except for meals and rest. 'It is all so real and true to me,' he told one correspondent, 'I believe the characters are living people.' The effort of course left him prostrate and exhausted. He felt like 'a washed-out rag'. He was taking calomel and colchicum and laudanum. He was also plagued by the further complication of angina that provoked the most painful sensations in his chest or what was known as 'breast pang'. These were only relieved by the inhalation of amyl nitrite which left him dizzy but without pain. Still he continued writing.

I Say No was another mystery of an inexplicable death. A young orphaned girl goes in search of the truth about her father's demise. She discovers that everyone from whom she seeks answers is, in fact, concealing an important element in the fatal story. Was her father murdered, his throat cut with a razor? The resolution is to be found in a bloodstained pocketbook which contains the words 'I say no'. So begins a compelling and almost irresistible narrative in the manner of Collins. It is a novel of pure suspense in which people come together, accidentally or coincidentally; they are linked by a deadly secret which only they can unravel. No one could plot this more finely than Collins himself.

And then his dog died. Tommy had been a constant companion for many years, and Collins was more desolate at this loss than at any time since the death of his brother; he said that he had suffered terribly during his pet's last illness. He had written in *The Fallen Leaves* that 'there are periods in a man's life when he finds the society that walks on four feet a welcome relief from the society that walks on two'. At night Tommy would come up to him, look at him, wag his tail, and groan; this was his signal that it was time to go to bed. Now he could walk nowhere and do nothing without missing the little Scottish terrier.

His spirits were lifted a little in the course of a curious correspondence with an eleven-year-old girl. He had met Nannie Wynne and her mother through the agency of Frank Beard, who was also their doctor. Collins was always immensely fond of children and their idiosyncrasies; some of the most charming moments of his fiction are devoted to them. He had the gift of an imaginative man in taking the conversations and the ideas of children entirely seriously.

The correspondence seems to have begun in the summer of 1885 and concluded in the spring of 1888. Collins's letters are couched in a teasing and affectionate style; he became her husband, and she was addressed as Mrs Wilkie Collins or 'Dear and admirable Mrs Collins'. 'This morning I had some red hot scratches again, and had to sniff at my "Amyl" (N.B. This is *not* the Christian name of a*not*her wife. It is only a glass capsule).' It was all perfectly innocent and demonstrates how quickly Collins could slip into a delightful fantasy life. It was perhaps the only way in which he could contemplate marriage.

19

That's Me

By the autumn of 1885 he was writing a drama and a novel simultaneously; they were essentially the same work but the laws of copyright meant that Collins had to make sure that the play was acted first in order to secure his rights. He believed that the story was essentially dramatic in spirit, and that to allow the 'pirates' to steal it for the stage was to remove much of its impact. He started work in Ramsgate, but was driven out by the noise of brass bands and costermongers selling fish; so he returned to the 'old work shop' of Gloucester Place. He really now seemed dedicated to his work, to the exclusion of almost everything else.

The Evil Genius began its newspaper syndication in December 1885, and Tillotson of the 'Fiction Bureau' paid him more for it than any previous book. There was no sense of a decline, at least in material fortunes. It has as its focus an unhappy household of man and wife with a young daughter. When an attractive governess enters the plot, the usual complications ensue. Governess leaves household but is called back when daughter pines for her; wife runs off with daughter and, after obtaining a Scottish divorce, goes into hiding. More complications and misunderstandings bring misery until husband and wife decide to remarry.

As always Collins concocts a complete nervous stew of people constantly afraid and constantly on the watch, relapsing into neuralgic fever, stealing each other's letters, running away from one another, terrified of nervous collapse or nervous paralysis; the two dominant passions are those of greed and of fear. This is also the atmosphere of the long story that Collins wrote after the completion of *The Evil Genius*. 'The Guilty River' was composed at high speed accompanied by all the signs of nervous anxiety and prostration. It is not clear what compulsion seized him at such times. It may have been in part the need for money as reassurance. It may have been the fear of idleness leading to a breakdown; a man who has been busily engaged in work for most of his life may look with horror upon the vacancy of free time. But it may also have been the compulsion of the storyteller. He said that 'The Guilty River' was knocking on his head and whispering, 'Why don't you let me out?'

He was working on the story twelve hours a day, and finished it within a month. It is the story of a deaf lodger, known as 'The Cur', who falls in love with his landlord's daughter and who tries to murder by poison a rival to her affections.

'Men of your age,' he resumed, 'seldom look below the surface. Learn that valuable habit, sir – and begin by looking below the surface of Me . . . Discover for yourself,' he said, 'what devils my deafness has set loose in me; and let no eyes but yours see that horrid sight. You will find me here tomorrow, and you will decide by that time whether you make an enemy of me or not.'

The stress of work of course ruined Collins's already fragile health once more. He told Nina Lehmann that, like the post-horses of a previous age, he had galloped along without feeling the strain. But 'do you remember how the forelegs of those post-horses quivered, and how their heads dropped, when they came to the journey's end? That's me, Padrona – that's me.' Or, as he put it to another correspondent, he was 'dead beat'; he felt weary, and old, and depressed. His brains were so addled after the effort that he did not know which end of him was uppermost.

In the course of this hard year, he was rarely 'at home' to casual visitors. The London fog was choking him. 'Did you wish you had never been born this morning?' he asked Watt. 'I did.' He could not sleep at night. He warned Edward Pigott about draughts in railway carriages. He was dying for the sight and the smell of the sea but, when he eventually reached Ramsgate in the summer of 1886, he was greeted by two thunderstorms and air almost too hot to breathe. When he was threatened once more with gout in the eye, he broke out in what he called 'a blue funk'. He was soon to suffer from a feverish cold in the London winter. The night air affected his chest. Nevertheless he still managed to get out. He took Caroline and Carrie to his box to see Lily Langtry in *The Lady of Lyons*, and was hoping to get to the Haymarket in the following week to see *Jim the Penman*. Theatre was like a drug to him. It took him out of the world.

The heat of the following summer induced in him a peculiar kind of nervous apprehension. He started when even a door was unexpectedly opened. He told a friend that, on the last occasion he had dined out, he had been 'sick with fright' every time the cab turned a corner. Beard had advised him to leave London, but he regarded with horror the prospect of any railway journey; the noise associated with it appalled him. The only remedy for him was a quiet night walk in a peaceful neighbourhood. When the air turned raw with winter, he became a prisoner at home.

He used to quote Samuel Johnson to the effect that 'what *must* be done *will* be done'. In that mood, therefore, he began work on what would be his last completed novel. *The Legacy of Cain* was serialised by Tillotson in various provincial newspapers but even as he was trying to keep up with the weekly episodes he was obliged to move house. His lease at Gloucester Place had run out and, in the face of exorbitant demands from his landlord, he looked for alternative accommodation in the neighbourhood.

He, or perhaps Caroline Graves, found the upper part of a house at 82 Wimpole Street and for the last time he endured the agonies of moving. He quoted the comments of his household. 'If you please, sir, I don't think the looking glass will fit in above the book-case in this house.' 'If the sideboard is put in the front drawing-room, we don't know where the cabinets are to go.' 'Here is the man, sir, with the patterns of wall-paper.' 'I beg your pardon, sir, did I understand that you wanted a lamp in the water-closet?' After two months the carpet had still not been laid in the dining room. And all the time he was only just keeping up with the flow of what the newspapers called 'copy'. The house did have its benefits, however. It was in a much quieter area than Gloucester Place; there was no mews at the back, only the storehouses of the traders of Wigmore Street.

He was not sure, when composing *The Legacy of Cain*, whether he was writing 'over the heads' of the contemporary public but it is not at all clear what he meant by that. It is essentially a drama of heredity and fate, including the key Collins elements of poison and attempted murder, madness and mistaken identity. Two young girls have been brought up together as sisters, although in fact one of them is an adopted orphan. The orphan is the daughter of a murderess who was executed for the savage murder of her husband; her 'sister' is the perfectly brought-up scion of a pious household. Which of them will turn to the bad? That is the legacy in question. There were many theories in the period on the nature of heredity, but Collins was essentially bored by theories. In this novel, as in the past, his most important concern is with the simple telling of the story.

Hall Caine was a visitor at Wimpole Street. He described Collins as quiet and a little nervous. 'He sat while he talked with his head half down, and his eyes usually on the table; but he looked into one's face from time to time, and his gaze was steady and encouraging.' His diffidence may have been a result of the exhaustion to which he was a prey.

When he attended a banquet held by the Society of Authors

in the summer of this year, 1888, however, he was anxious to know who were the new celebrities in the world of literature. It is not known to whom he was introduced, but his opinion of the 'up and coming' writers was not necessarily high. He remarked that, according to the newspapers, seven or eight 'great geniuses' were to be celebrated every week. On a literary feud currently being conducted in the public prints, he commented only that 'these wretched creatures are completely saturated with self-conceit'. One of his characters in *The Evil Genius* remarks of 'new writers' that they provide 'no story to excite our poor nerves; no improper characters to cheat us of our sympathies; no dramatic situations to frighten us; exquisite management of details (as the reviews say) and a masterly anatomy of human motives which – I know what I mean, my dear, but I can't explain it'.

Of all the younger writers he seems most to have admired Rider Haggard, whose *King Solomon's Mines* and *She* amply followed his example of forcefully telling a story. He never mentions Henry James or Thomas Hardy, but he did say that he enjoyed the first half of Robert Louis Stevenson's *Kidnapped*. He had what might be called old-fashioned tastes.

At the beginning of 1889, having left a dinner party, he hired a four-horse cab. Just as it was coming out into Knightsbridge it collided with another vehicle; his cab tipped over, and bits of glass covered him. He went flying out of the upper door and fortunately landed on the pavement without a bruise. He had also been uninjured by the glass, but he was shaken. It was not a good omen for the year. He was soon suffering from neuralgic attacks that could only be soothed by tablespoonfuls of laudanum.

He was still, however, eager to begin another novel. He said his invention was 'boiling' with new characters and new stories. *Blind Love* was in part concerned with a great insurance fraud recently uncovered in Germany; a man takes out a life insurance policy but then ensures that a dying man, closely resembling him, takes his place in a hospital. The poor man's death was then hastened by poison. Collins combined this plot with the story of the obsessive love of a good-hearted woman for a rogue. It has all the ingredients of his later fiction.

By 21 June he marked on the manuscript that 'the story, so far, has been written for press to the end of Part 18'. Nine days later he suffered a stroke; his left side was paralysed and it was feared that his brain had also been affected. Frank Beard arrived and determined to stay the night. He was conscious at intervals, but had some 'suffocation' about the heart. Carrie Graves wrote to Watt that 'he is light-headed at times, and does not know how ill he is'. He was also 'hyper-excited' with anxiety about the progress of the novel. He did not know, but may have guessed, that he would not work on it again. A month later Carrie Graves reported him to be gaining in strength, but she mentioned that the 'paralysis' was still affecting his brain. She wrote to the novelist Mary Elizabeth Braddon that 'it is a terrible shock – to see such a wonderful genius struck down in an instant'. He was more composed than before, however, and was talking a great deal about the past; she told the novelist that 'it makes your heart ache to see and hear him'.

On 4 August he suffered a relapse, and was unable to eat or drink for twenty-six hours. But then he rallied once more, and Caroline was able to take breakfast with him. He seemed much revived, and Carrie took her children to Brighton; two paid nurses were still in the house. At the end of the month he dictated a letter by means of his oldest daughter, Marian, to Watt in which he reported that the doctor was content with his progress. It was Watt who relieved his anxieties over the unfinished *Blind Love* by persuading another novelist, Walter Besant, to complete it for him. It was not as difficult a task as it might seem since Collins, according to his familiar practice, had sketched out every twist and turn of the plot in great detail; he had also composed some of the dialogue. 'I was much struck', Besant wrote, 'with the writer's perception of the vast importance of dialogue in making the reader seize the scene.' The serialisation had begun in the *Illustrated London News* on 6 July and continued uninterrupted until the end.

By the beginning of September Collins's hand was steady enough to write a letter to Frederick Lehmann in which he announced that the doctor was 'hopeful' and that he himself looked forward to 'healthier days'. He was too weak to see all of the visitors who came to Wimpole Street but he did manage to converse with George Redford, who used to play the cello at George Eliot's musical evenings. Redford later recalled that 'he said as he grasped my hand with all his old warmth, "you see I'm alright – feel my arm".' He and Redford then smoked a cigar together. Redford added that 'I had hard work to hide my eyes'. An attack of bronchitis then intervened, two weeks later, and he was huddled up by the fire wrapped in blankets. On 21 September he scribbled a note in pencil to Frank Beard. 'I am *dying* old friend. W.C.' Then, on a separate piece of paper, he jotted down another message. 'They are driving me mad *by forbidding* the Hy . . . Come for God's sake. I am too wretched to write.' Hy . . . might be the beginning of hypodermic. Beard came at once but now his patient was beyond the help of any earthly agency. He sank slowly and without pain. In her diary for Monday, 23 September, Caroline Graves wrote that 'Wilkie died at 10 a.m.'

20

A Postscript

The funeral party gathered at Wimpole Street on the morning of Friday 27 September to accompany the hearse on its journey to Kensal Green Cemetery. Among the mourners were William Holman-Hunt and Edward Pigott from his youthful days; Charles Dickens junior and Frank Beard were there, together with Arthur Pinero and Squire Bancroft. Andrew Chatto and Alexander Watt joined them. Caroline Graves, with Carrie Bartley and her husband, represented the official family. Martha Rudd and her children were not present at the service. Instead a cross of white chrysanthemums was sent 'from Mrs Dawson and family'. Collins despised Victorian conventions to the end; he ordered that there should be no black hatbands or feathers or funeral scarves.

In his will he divided his estate equally between Caroline Graves and Carrie Bartley, and Martha Rudd with her children by him. Despite his composition of twenty-one novels and seventeen plays he did not die a very rich man, leaving an estate of a little under £11,000. Caroline Graves took care of the grave at Kensal Green until her own death in 1895 placed her in the same earth. Martha Rudd then tended the grave until her death in 1919.

The Major Works of Wilkie Collins

Memoirs of the Life of William Collins R.A. (1848)
Basil (1852)
Hide and Seek (1854)
The Dead Secret (1857)
The Woman in White (1860)
No Name (1862)
Armadale (1866)
The Moonstone (1868)
Man and Wife (1870)
The New Magdalen (1873)
The Law and the Lady (1875)
A Rogue's Life (volume publication) (1879)
The Fallen Leaves (1879)
Heart and Science (1883)
I Say No (1884)

Bibliography

Ashley, Robert: *Wilkie Collins* (London, 1952)

Bachman, Maria K. and Cox, Don Richard (eds): *Reality's Dark Light: The Sensational Wilkie Collins* (Knoxville, TN, 2003)

Baker, William: *Wilkie Collins's Library* (Westport, CT, 2002)

Baker, William and Clarke, William M. (eds): *The Letters of Wilkie Collins*, in two volumes (London, 1999)

Baker, William, Gasson, Andrew, Law, Graham and Lewis, Paul (eds): *The Public Face of Wilkie Collins: The Collected Letters*, in four volumes (London, 2005)

Clarke, William M.: *The Secret Life of Wilkie Collins* (London, 1988)

Davis, Nuel Pharr: *The Life of Wilkie Collins* (Urbana, IL, 1956)

Drinkwater, John (ed.): *The Eighteen-Sixties* (Cambridge, 1932)

Ellis, S. M.: *Wilkie Collins, Le Fanu and Others* (London, 1951)

Gasson, Andrew: *Wilkie Collins: An Illustrated Guide* (Oxford, 1998)

Grinstein, Alexander: *Wilkie Collins* (Madison, CT, 2003)

Law, Graham and Maunder, Andrew: *Wilkie Collins: A Literary Life* (London, 2008)

Lonoff, Sue: *Wilkie Collins and his Victorian Readers* (New York, 1982)

Nayder, Lillian: *Wilkie Collins* (New York, 1997)

Nayder, Lillian: *Unequal Partners: Charles Dickens, Wilkie Collins and Victorian Authorship* (London, 2002)

O'Neill, Philip: *Wilkie Collins* (London, 1988)

Page, Norman (ed.): *Wilkie Collins: The Critical Heritage* (London, 1974)

Peters, Catherine: *The King of Inventors* (London, 1991)

Pykett, Lyn: *Wilkie Collins* (Oxford, 2005)

Robinson, Kenneth: *Wilkie Collins* (London, 1974)

Sayers, Dorothy L.: *Wilkie Collins* (Toledo, OH, 1977)

Smith, Nelson and Terry, R. C. (eds): *Wilkie Collins to the Forefront* (New York, 1995)

Taylor, Jenny Bourne: *In the Secret Theatre of Home* (London, 1988)

Taylor, Jenny Bourne (ed.): *The Cambridge Companion to Wilkie Collins* (Cambridge, 2006)

Thompson, Julian (ed.): *Wilkie Collins: The Complete Shorter Fiction* (London, 1995)

Index

NOTE: Works by Wilkie Collins (WC) appear directly under title; works by others under author's name